THE CLEAVAGE IN OUR CULTURE

Max Otto

THE CLEAVAGE
IN OUR CULTURE

Studies in Scientific Humanism in Honor of

MAX OTTO

Edited by Frederick Burkhardt

Essay Index Reprint Series

BOOKS FOR LIBRARIES PRESS
FREEPORT, NEW YORK

STANDARD BOOK NUMBER:

8369-1396-5

LIBRARY OF CONGRESS CATALOG CARD NUMBER:

74-90619

PRINTED IN THE UNITED STATES OF AMERICA

Contents

Preface

In 1947, when Max Otto retired from his active and distinguished teaching of philosophy at the University of Wisconsin, a number of his friends and colleagues began writing to one another about rendering him some testimony of their regard for him and his influence as a thinker, teacher, and friend.

It took some time for a book to emerge from these informal and spontaneous beginnings—much longer than it would have taken if the organization had been official and formal. Boyd Bode finally crystallized the project after a conversation with John Dewey, by writing the piece which sets the theme of the present volume and sending it off to the man who, in dealing with it, found himself fairly naturally, and almost without being aware of it, in the position of editor.

For a time, while the editor was abroad, Horace S. Fries took over the manuscript. He induced G. C. Sellery, a close friend and colleague of Max Otto at Wisconsin, to write the Biographical Note, and handled a great many onerous arrangements for publication. The death of Horace Fries in 1951, at the height of his powers, was a tragic loss to contemporary philosophy. His contribution to the present volume was so large in both ideas and energy that his name might well have appeared not only as a contributor but also as an editor.

I should also like to acknowledge a large debt to George R. Geiger, who took over as custodian of the project and kept it going in its semi-final stages.

So now, after more than the normal vicissitudes of a co-operative work, we have brought forth this book. We hope we have avoided

some of the deadlier aspects of the *Festschrift*. At least every essay
in the book was written especially for it and not retrieved from some
store of unpublished manuscripts, and every writer in the volume is
a personal friend of Max Otto's who not only understands what he
has been up to all these years but has been affected by his thinking.
This has, we hope, resulted in a homogeneity of spirit and outlook,
even though the fields represented, besides philosophy, include psychology, education, mathematics, social work, and economics.

The other kind of unity—unity of theme—is also present. Although the contributors are not confined to professional philosophers, the volume is a consistent expression of the modern naturalism known as Scientific Humanism, and either explicitly or implicitly this way of thinking is brought to bear on the problem set
by Boyd Bode in the first chapter. Each contributor was sent that
original chapter and asked to apply his special competence to
some aspect of the problem there set forth. No further editorial
strictures were considered necessary. The philosophical homogeneity of the contributors and their shared motivation took care
of the rest. John Dewey, taking the initial theme, defined the function of philosophy within a one-world outlook, and Horace Kallen
elaborated the conception of truth which it must accept. Two of the
contributors, Arnold Dresden and Norman Cameron, surveyed
their own disciplines (mathematics and psychiatry) for methodological leads which promise to be fruitful if applied to the fields
of social science and ethics. The chapters of Eduard C. Lindeman,
Horace S. Fries, and George R. Geiger are examples of the new
function of philosophy which Dewey has called for in his essay:
"building up a sense of the frame of reference, the kind of standpoint and of outlook, in which human problems are to be specified,
and hypotheses for their resolution projected and tested." A. Eustace
Haydon, Harold Taylor, and C. E. Ayres in their chapters have
developed the implications and consequences of the theme of the
volume in the fields of religion, education, and economics.

To this extent the reader will find the book a unified, coherent expression of a modern philosophical point of view. It makes no claim,

however, to be a complete and systematic exposition of it, nor has it included all of the fields of knowledge and endeavor, such as art, law, labor, public administration, and many others, which might have been brought into a more definitive book. Max Otto has students and friends in all of them and there is ample and acknowledged evidence of the effect of his thinking in their work. Justice and thoroughness argued for their inclusion, but reasons of health, time, or other responsibilities have, as this volume was prepared, prevented their taking up their rightful option. And since, as such things go, this book was already long in being born, the editorial fiat was imposed, the deadline set and—here it is—a collection of essays around a theme which has been of central interest in Max Otto's philosophizing. The contributors hope that he, and the reader, will find in it some contribution to the making of the kind of "One World" for which he has worked so brilliantly these many years.

FREDERICK BURKHARDT

Bennington College
Bennington, Vermont

THE CLEAVAGE IN OUR CULTURE

I

The Cleavage in Our Culture

BOYD H. BODE

Professor Emeritus of Education, Ohio State University

During recent years there have been occasional opportunities to witness a strange spectacle. It is the spectacle of man surveying his achievements in the field of the physical sciences until he becomes afraid of himself. Homilies on man's proneness to evil because of his ignorance and gullibility are no new thing; but this is something different. It now appears that the time has come to view with alarm, for the curious reason that man has been so signally successful in devising ways and means for discovering truth and protecting himself against error. Man equipped with science gives promise—so the prophets of doom feel impelled to warn us—of becoming his own worst enemy. If progress in science continues, it may mean the destruction of our civilization.

Opposition to science is of course something with which the world has long been familiar. The experience of Galileo is a case in point. But Galileo was suppressed on the ground that he taught an erroneous doctrine, and not for revealing a truth that had better be kept dark. The present fear is that the truth will destroy us, unless we can keep it in abeyance long enough to establish external, moral controls. The atomic bomb is a dramatic illustration of what we may expect unless we watch our step.

All this is very confusing. It seems to say that the domain of scientific knowledge is so completely separate from the domain of

3

moral standards and ideals that each is foreign territory to the other. The fact that scientific knowledge is so readily convertible into technological applications is indeed evidence that it is quite capable of generating aims and purposes on its own account. But these aims and purposes are declared to be lacking in moral quality unless this moral quality is imported from the outside, for the purpose of maintaining the right kind of control. Moral authority thus becomes an external thing. Its credentials are not subject to the same kind of examination and testing as that which we apply elsewhere; which is to say that moral insight must be attained along a different road. Something of this kind is clearly implied in the forlorn suggestion that a moratorium should be declared in the natural sciences so as to give our moral insight a chance to catch up.

Here is a cleavage of the first magnitude. How did it originate? From all accounts primitive man was spared this affliction—whether it was because he had no science or for some other reason. His pattern for living appears to have had no serious cracks in it and to have been reasonably adequate for his needs. From the vantage point of the twentieth century we can hazard a suggestion why this was so. The test for right living in his case was based on the requirements for membership in his group. It was in and through such membership that he secured opportunity for the development of his personal capacities. Loyalty to the common life of his group was identical with loyalty to his personal interests and needs. This is not to say, of course, that primitive man was disposed to base his beliefs and conduct on philosophical reflection. His loyalty was a spontaneous product. As a rule the identification of himself with his group was doubtless taken for granted, since familiarity is easily mistaken for reasonableness. If justification was required, the demands on his loyalty could be defended on the ground that they were useful or that they had the approval of the gods.

Eventually, however, such justification was bound to become more difficult, for the reason that the basis for the common life consisted mainly of tradition and custom. Loyalty to the common life, therefore, led inevitably to conflicts wherever it became evident that tradition and custom failed to take account of changes in conditions and growth in knowledge and experiences. This development was dramatically illustrated in ancient Greece by the rise of the Sophists, who in some cases challenged the authority of tradition altogether. In doing so, however, they failed to recognize the necessity of membership in a group and so unwittingly poured out the baby with the bath. What they thought they proved was that morality was an outworn superstition; what they really proved was that tradition and custom did not constitute 'an adequate basis for loyalty to a common life. In order to be entitled to such loyalty, morality had to be provided with a more secure foundation.

The search for such a foundation was begun by Socrates and continued by Plato. In retrospect it is not difficult to see the limitations under which Plato approached the problem or to admire the ingenuity and daring through which he arrived at a solution. Tradition and custom were admittedly inadequate. For Plato this meant that the world of everyday affairs, which was conducted on the basis of custom and the accumulation of piecemeal, empirical experiences, had nothing relevant to offer. So he turned instead to the activities of the intelligentsia, the aristocratic class, which cultivated pursuits that were divorced from practical affairs and directed toward insight into the true, the good, and the beautiful. The line between the two kinds of activity being thus sharply drawn, Plato advanced the breath-taking theory that man is simultaneously a denizen of two different worlds. One of these worlds is the world of everyday experience, a world of space and time. The other is a realm of supersensuous, eternal and immutable reality, which lies beyond space and time and which furnishes us with standards for belief and conduct. In brief, Plato converted the type of social organization in which he lived into a metaphysical theory of two-worldism. In so doing he met the challenge of the Sophists for a more firm foundation for moral values, but at the price of making morality a form of control which is imposed upon everyday life from the outside. In providing a metaphysical basis for this external control,

Plato became the father of a cleavage in our culture which has haunted us down to the present day.

In a sense, Plato's solution proved to be a feasible working hypothesis. At any rate it was adopted by Christian theology and thus managed to keep itself in a dominant position throughout all the succeeding centuries, with the result that it became firmly imbedded in our Western culture. Nevertheless, the relations between the two worlds established by the Platonic philosophy turned out to be in a constant state of unstable equilibrium, for the reason that the world of practical affairs, which had been placed in a position subordinate to the realm of transcendental and immutable reality, was always pressing against the restrictions that were placed upon it. In politics it became the issue of government by divine right against government "with the consent of the governed." In economics it led to the conflict between the alleged sanctity of "free enterprise" and the desirability of governmental control. In theology it took the form of state responsibility for the purity of doctrine as over against freedom of conscience and freedom of inquiry. In education it became the problem of the competing claims of "culture" and "practical" subjects. The history of "progress" in our Western civilization is a record of the struggle to widen the domain of the "practical" life by giving it greater autonomy in determining its own standards and ideals. Since the struggle was directed against external control, "liberty" and "democracy" became favorite watchwords in the ranks of the discontented.

On the whole, the stars in their courses have been on the side of progress in this sense of the term. Concession after concession has had to be made to new demands. It is significant, however, that the concessions were generally made without surrender of the basic philosophy of two-worldism. The concessions took the form of adjustments *within* the traditional framework. The political struggle, for example, led to theories about "inalienable rights" with which the individual was endowed by the creator and which, therefore, likewise had a transcendental source; the theological struggle, with its slogan of "every man his own priest," became a question of the interpretation of priesthood; the claims of "experience" as over against reason or revelation culminated in theories about "sensation" and "intellect." The soul of Plato was still marching on.

To put it differently, the fundamental issue hardly ever emerged in clear-cut form. The real question was not how or where the line should be drawn between the "empirical" and the "transcendental" realms, after the pattern of Platonism, but whether any such line should be drawn at all. The failure to raise this question has serious consequences, in that it prevented the realm of everyday experience from developing its own ideals and standards. The Reformation, for example, insisted on giving more scope to the intelligence and conscience of the individual person, as over against the claims of an established church. It thus widened the domain of the "secular" at the expense of the "sacred" or the "transcendental." It did not, however, challenge the doctrine that standards and ideals had to be imported from this outside world, and so the movement tended to gravitate to the level of a quarrel among theologians. Similarly the American Revolution, which likewise undertook to trim down the claims of "divine right" so as to give more authority to the common man, was not prepared to go the whole way and define the rights and duties of the citizen in terms of purely social relationships. The standards were again imported from the outside under the label of "inalienable rights." "The trail of the serpent was over it all."

The net result of all this was that the trend towards the autonomy and enrichment of "secular" living—which is about what we mean by democracy—became saddled with an assortment of little absolutes, which cramped its style considerably. Such concepts as "freedom of conscience," "free speech," and "inalienable rights," for example, established themselves as "eternal truths," after the manner of the Platonic tradition, which meant that they did not have to justify themselves in terms of circumstance and function. In practice no specific rights are inalienable, and no freedoms can be permitted to disregard limiting conditions. How then are they to be interpreted and applied? A cynic might say that men struggle long and desperately for certain rights, only to find that they do not know what to do with them after they have got them.

The conflict therefore continues. It is presumably obvious that such concepts as liberty, democracy, equality, and the public good do not come to us with a set of directions to show how they are to be interpreted and applied. By implication, therefore, we find ourselves constantly involved in the "fundamental issue." It makes all the difference in the world whether we deal with such concepts within the framework of two-worldism or outside of it. In the former case there is no escape from the necessity of relying on experts who can speak with authority on matters pertaining to eternal truth. Plato recognized this necessity by providing different types of education for an upper and a lower class, and thus setting a pattern which has come down to us through the centuries in the form of the familiar contrast between culture and vocation. The medieval church made the clergy the final court of appeal and so got started on a type of interpretation which has become known as casuistry. Thus is maintained the principle of external control, which is basically a form of "thought control," and constitutes a denial of the view that ordinary experience can generate its own standards and ideals.

The trend away from two-worldism, however, appears to be gaining momentum. This is due in large part to the fact that we are beginning to feel the full impact of scientific method in thinking and also the effect of the changes which have been wrought by the application of science to the conditions under which we live. The tradition of two-worldism is being strained to the breaking point. Ordinary experience has become equipped with the methods and the results of science, with the consequence that the attempt to hold it in the leading strings of a metaphysical theory about reality threatens to become an absurdity. Science as science recognizes no such distinctions as are implied in the doctrine of two-worldism. It has always shown a disposition to ignore the landmarks which were supposed to separate the secular from the sacred or the natural from the supernatural. It has dared, for example, to try to deflect the lightning by means of lightning rods, to ward off epidemics through inoculations, to disregard the order of nature by street lighting, to replace the doctrine of original sin as an explanation of wrongdoing by having recourse to the organic relationship between individual and environment as an explanation of behavior. Its success and its prestige have become so great that many who are still under the influence of the two-world tradition are puzzled to know where to draw the line.

It has become a commonplace to say that we are living in a period of transition. The new wine is playing havoc with the old bottles. The present situation is new in the sense that the realm of "ordinary experience" is becoming more and more autonomous and correspondingly less and less amenable to the external controls which spring from the traditional framework of two-worldism. If traffic rules, for example, can be generated from the requirements of free co-operation among men, why should not such matters as divorce or birth control be determined on the same basis? We are in a period of transition because the incompatibility between the old and the new is becoming more acute. This incompatibility is becoming evident inside the churches as well as outside of them. We have long been familiar with the opposition to emphasis on creeds in theological circles. The weakness of that movement is that it is content to dilute or obscure the authority of two-worldism, instead of re-examining its basis. There is much current talk about democracy as a "way of life," but there is little recognition of the fact that democracy as a way of life means by implication the repudiation of two-worldism as a basis for moral standards and ideals. The consequence of all this is that we continue to derive these standards and ideals from two different and discordant conceptions of what constitutes a good life, and thus inevitably land in confusion. There probably never was a generation that knew so much and yet so little as is the case at the present time. There is no way out of this confusion except to re-examine our past in order to determine whether two-worldism can claim to have more than a historical justification.

To put it simply, there is an alternative to the Platonic doctrine of two-worldism which should have our careful consideration. As a point of departure we may grant, fully and unreservedly, that traditions and custom do not provide an adequate basis for moral beliefs and conduct. This, however, does not mean that we have to choose between the Sophists and Plato. Tradition and custom had a limited justification in the fact that membership in the community is an indispensable condition if the individual is to become human at all. Participation in a common life is essential. If this be conceded, we have a basis both for recognizing the authority of tradition and custom and also for judging of their shortcomings. Tradition and custom, even if followed blindly, lead to a certain measure of participation, but they may also operate to obstruct wider participation —in such ways, for example, as keeping women in their place, perpetuating the institution of slavery, and justifying the exploitation of the masses by a ruling class. When this becomes obvious, the alternative is not to repudiate moral standards, nor yet to justify these standards by having recourse to a transcendental realm, but to modify the pattern of living, whatever it may be, so as to secure constant widening of participation. The continuity of experience is thus preserved and a principle for the guidance of conduct is provided. Tradition and custom are recognized for what they are, viz., as gateways for sharing in a common life. Their authority, however, is not absolute. This recognition carries the implication that the moral life does not require either unquestioning conformity to the pattern of living which happens to prevail at any given place or time or the notion that it derives its authority from a fourth dimension, but is based on the proposition that morality finds its fulfillment in the continuous extension of common interests and common purposes among men.

The issue confronting the present generation is the same as it was in the days of Plato. It is again a question of providing an adequate basis for the moral life. For the sake of the argument, if nothing else, we may grant that Plato took the only course that was open to him as an alternative to moral anarchy. At any rate, we now have resources available to us which were not available in those earlier times. In considering the question of moral values, the modern man can draw upon a vast fund of material, placed at his disposal by such subjects as anthropology, psychology, and sociology, to say nothing of the "lessons of history," with its dreary record of fanaticism and intolerance and its endless twisting of the traditional framework of two-worldism in order to accommodate some special interest or point of view. It is fairly clear that the mundane world of "practical experience" has grown steadily in power and in the disposition to organize itself in its own way, despite the attempt to maintain external controls. This is, of course, precisely as it should be if we identify morality with the continuous extension of common interests and purposes. Morality, in that case, has its origin wholly within the social relations among men and provides its own empirical tests of right and wrong, without having recourse to "absolute truths" of any kind.[1]

In one way or another, all the basic questions of the present age trace back to this issue of morality. Our moral values are either purely social in their origin and validity or else they derive their credentials from some different source. Fundamentally the issue is as simple as that. The attitude of two-worldism, however, has become so deeply ingrained in our habits of thinking that it has proved difficult to get the issue out into the open. Scientists, who—like everyone else—have been brought up in the tradition of two-worldism, have been disposed to regard morality as something unrelated to science or else to undertake in their later years to explain how science can be reconciled with "religion," which was usually identified with two-worldism. In either case they have given their sanction to the perpetuation of the cleavage in our culture.

It is hardly to be expected that the framework of two-worldism will soon be superseded by an outlook of a different kind. We shall

---

[1] For an exceptionally able and readable elaboration of this general point of view, the reader is referred to Max Otto's *Things and Ideals,* especially Chapter 3 ("Right for Right's Sake"); Chapter 5 ("Right by Agreement"); and Chapter 12 ("The Hunger for Cosmic Support"). Cf. also Chapter 5 of *The Human Enterprise,* by the same author.

doubtless continue to search for "reconciliations," in order to maintain the agelong habit of living simultaneously in two different worlds, despite the fact that it gives every indication of leading us into philosophical bankruptcy. Man has become afraid of himself because he is losing his sense of direction. Instead of gaining courage from his success through the use of scientific method, he takes for granted that he is required to maintain the cleavage in our culture. He thus deprives himself of the only effective means at his disposal for building a kingdom of heaven on earth and makes himself ridiculous by talking about a moratorium on science in order that the blueprints for such a kingdom may be provided by metaphysics or theology.

To the student this development affords a striking illustration of the function of habit in social living, and it also explains why the spectacular revolutions recorded for us in history so often appear to be mostly surface phenomena. The French have a saying: "The more change, the more it is the same thing." To be enduring, the changes that take place must be founded on changes in our collective habits of thinking and acting, and such changes cannot be wrought overnight by proclamation or by changes in the machinery of government. The immediate effect is likely to take the form of "reconciliations," which are usually devices for holding the changes in basic habits or outlook to a minimum. This is the price that we pay for preserving the continuity of our common life. But it is a stiff price if it obscures the significance of the changes that have occurred. In the present case the conflict is nothing less than a conflict between basic theories of moral values, or between competing philosophies of life.

It is true, no doubt, that this conflict reaches far back into the past. There have always been complaints that "spiritual" standards are being ignored and that life is becoming "secularized." But in this age of science and technology the issue is becoming much more acute and the resulting confusion is becoming correspondingly ominous. This confusion is the greatest threat to our national ideal of democracy. We cannot have it both ways. Either democracy is a way of life which can generate its own standards and ideals from purely social relationships and thus maintain its own distinctive system of ethics, or else democracy must be trimmed down so as to make it fit into a transcendental or metaphysical framework and thus be deprived of the claim that it represents a distinctive way of life.

It is precisely on this issue that academic philosophy has been so largely disappointing. By and large its efforts have been devoted chiefly to the task of maintaining the Platonic tradition by making such adjustments as might be required in a changing world. Instead of challenging the original dualism between the sensuous and the supersensuous, it has resorted to the device of inventing further dualisms for the purpose of making the first one good. Thus, the dualism of two worlds clearly called for a corresponding dualism between knowledge derived from sense perception on the one hand and knowledge derived from reason or revelation or intuition on the other. It called for a dualism between "practical" knowledge, which creates its own standards and its own tests, and "theoretical" knowledge, which operates differently or which provides us with absolute truths. It called for a dualism between the "subject" that is trying to know his environment and the "object" to be known. Kant's famous remark about the starry heavens above and the moral law within summarizes this situation. It postulates a knower with one eye focused on the outside world and the other on the recesses of his own bosom, and thus dramatizes both the difference in the two kinds of knowing and the difficulty in securing a solid foundation for either kind. It led inevitably to the epistemological problem of how knowledge is possible at all, which—if we avoid the original dualism—is of interest chiefly as an occupational disease of philosophers.

The dualisms just mentioned are characteristic of technical philosophy, but the matter does not end there. In education the original dualism turns up as a hard and fast contrast between culture and vocation. In law it takes the form of the opposition between the authority of precedent or "natural law" and the requirements of expediency. In economics we encounter it as a separation between economic and moral considerations. In political theory it becomes an opposition between the "individual" and "society." The over-all result is that we are now beginning to talk about a moratorium in science in order to keep our troubles within bounds. A better plan would be to re-examine the dualism in which these troubles have their origin. What God hath joined together, let not man put asunder.

2

Modern Philosophy

JOHN DEWEY

Late Professor of Philosophy, Columbia University

THE EXPRESSION "MODERN PHILOSOPHY" has two senses. "Modern" stands for a period of time; it also stands for what marks off the systems of the last few centuries from Greco-Roman and medieval systems. This negative demarcation is more accurate than one which is positive. For in the scene presented to us, little community can be found in the conclusions that have been reached. There is rather an exhibit of diverse and competing views. Such unity as exists is in the type of *problems* dealt with in their sharply marked difference from those of ancient and medieval times. Concern with issues that are formulated as dualisms is a report of extensive oppositions in life itself. This report is the distinguishing stamp of the accomplishments of modern philosophical discussion. It is notable that the modern system most ambitiously aiming at unity found its way to final complete unification on a road that was surveyed and laid out by the movement of contrarieties.

The postulates of the pages that follow are that (1) the dualisms which are the staple of modern philosophy are, in the first place, reflections, mirrorings, of clashes, cleavages in the cultural life of the West; and that (2) these splits and divisions are manifestations of the impact of new movements in science, industry, the arts generally, in religion and political organization, upon institutions having deep roots in the past. The new movements gave a profound

15

shock to established institutions, but they did not overthrow them. The vision of a new world was opened, literally, through exploration, discovery, and migration; and, symbolically, in the new astronomy and physics. But in respect to concerns and values that were fundamental the vision that was congenial to the old world persisted. It had been generated and shaped in the customs and usages of untold centuries. This vision of two unlike worlds is the distinctive mark of philosophy that is modern in other than a chronological sense. Its specific expression is the dualisms with which philosophy has wrestled.

In the first phase of the modern movement, the deviation from the old assumed the guise of return—of restoration of what was even more ancient. This phase is recorded in the names by which they are called—Renaissance, Revival of Learning, Reformation. But because of the intensity of the shock of old institutions by the new tendencies, the Reformation became the Protestant Revolt; the Revival of Learning passed into the Scientific Revolution; then came the Industrial and Political Revolutions. The fact that modern philosophies are the report of these changes does not signify that all of them were committed to the new. It means that everywhere philosophic inquiry was so sensitive to the breaks and cleavages that were introduced as to undertake reconciliations, adjustments, accommodations, compromises. But whatever mode was resorted to and wherever emphasis fell, the issues were of divisions formulated as dualisms.

The latter are so conspicuous that they come readily to mind: The material and spiritual; the physical and the mental or psychical; body and mind; experience and reason; sense and intellect; appetitive desire and will; subjective and objective; individual and social; inner and outer—this last division underlying in a way all the others. For the old presented itself to the adherents of the new movements as something external to what was vital and intimate; the inner was expressed in and supported by personal conscience, by private consciousness, by intuition—things set over against institutional pressures coming from "without." Seen in retrospect, however, all of the above terms are reflections of an underlying institutional, collective event, which may be roughly summed up as an invasion of the sacred by the secular.

In comprehensive retrospect, it also looks as if the great mass, the "common people," viewed the new not as in conflict with the old, but as its enlargement, as an added source of enjoyment. In effect, put in words, its attitude was: "Let us make the best of both worlds, this and the next." Members of the intellectual class were, however, compelled to take sides. Some of them fought for the right of the new science to a recognized place; others felt an obligation to defend the old from the encroaching impact of the new. The most overt and obvious clash bears the name "The Warfare of Science and Religion." Its details are now chiefly of historic interest. But it probably better expresses the core of the problems that lie back of the dualisms which philosophers formulated than does any other clash.

To those engaged in defense of the old, the very heart of the conflict was within science itself. For a passing glance at the old science, which had been pervasively absorbed into medieval theology as its intellectual structure, discloses how destructive was the new, incoming natural science. The old "science" was in fact a cosmology, in which the word *cosmos* is to be understood literally—that is, as a name for a harmoniously ordered, well-proportioned, and immutably defined (or finite) systematic whole, whose natural, or proper, culmination was Reason as Logos, *Ratio*. Changes occurred and produced excess and deficit in measure. But they were kept within fixed bonds by an immanent Logos. Science, as human knowing, was itself the realized manifestation of the immutable order of nature. Because of the adoption of this system into the structural scheme of Christian faith, this "science" had become its backbone. While nature had been deeply marred and corrupted by the Sin of Man, it remained the solid substance of the true knowing of "science," and supernatural agencies promised its ultimate restoration by means of divine intervention.

The effect of the new astronomy and physics was definitely disruptive; it was more than a shock in science. It profoundly disturbed the moral-religious convictions and institutions that had saturated for generations the imagination and emotions of man in the Western world. The crisis in which modern philosophy developed was, in short, broadly and deeply cultural, not technical. It is not necessary to do more than mention the total incompatibility of the new science with the old, long-accepted, and deeply embedded cosmology. The measure of things that had been fixed by proportions of an artistic nature gave way to the measure of quantities, which in the earlier scheme had been matters of excess and deficiency occasioned by "accidents," which entered in but did not disturb the order of the whole. Motions took the place occupied earlier by control of movements by the Immutable. The "material" causation that had occupied a subordinate place in the old science was replaced by the all-important "efficient causation." "Final Causes," the Ends, which controlled changes tending by their own nature to fulfill purposes, were relegated to theology. What had been accident, contingency, in the earlier scheme became the necessary mechanistic structure of the natural world.

When one views the completeness of the intellectual disruption involved in the new physics, one may be surprised that its consequences were not more catastrophic than was actually the case. But the logic of accommodation in the "practical" affairs of life is stronger than the logic of theoretical consistency. Events actually moved in the direction that was taken (as has been previously stated) by the mass of men, who were more concerned with immediate practical matters than with theories which to them were far away. That is to say, events moved intellectually as well as practically toward a division of fields, and a division of jurisdiction between authorities placed in control of the two fields. Conflict was prevented because, by common consent, the two "domains" touched but did not overlap. The higher was spiritual, ideal; it was supreme —provided it did not intrude too inconveniently on ordinary, everyday, secular affairs. The lower was the range of weekday occupations and concerns that were permitted to go their own way—

provided they rendered due obeisance to the purely ideal supremacy of the spiritual.

Just as political revolutions are never as total and final in their immediate occurrence as they seem to both adherents and opponents, so in the case of the scientific, industrial, and political "revolutions" arising from the impact of the new upon the old. At every point, the newer movements were deflected and more or less arrested by injection of elements that represent the actively operating presence of the old. In consequence, the dualism which is probably the most fundamental of all the dualisms with which modern philosophy deals is one that is rarely mentioned. It is the split between philosophy and science. In the Greek and medieval periods, philosophy *was* science in the complete and ultimate sense of Knowledge. It was at once the apex, the culmination, of all other sciences, and their sure and unchangeable basis and guarantee. In the basic dualism of scientific and philosophic subject matters, philosophy became the owner, guardian, and defender of the interests, activities, and values that had been violently expelled from science. Baser "material" activities and concerns were assigned to natural science. And as the prestige of the supernatural declined, philosophy took over the office of rational justification of those higher values that were no longer taken care of by science, and whose guarantee by revelation from on high was becoming precarious.

II

There are signs that we have now reached a state where conditions demand a marked change in both the subject matter and the office that have been assigned to philosophy, and which, in pointing the way to the kind of change that is needed, also supply the means, the instrumentalities, by which it is to be carried into effect. It is perhaps too extreme to say that philosophy today is in a state of doldrums—in the dictionary sense in which doldrums "are the state in which a ship makes no headway because of calm or contrary winds." But only optimists, who at best are not numerous, would say that philosophy is making great headway at present.

Discussions of such issues as Empiricism *versus* Rationalism, Realism *versus* Idealism, were warm and eager hardly more than a generation ago. They have now almost disappeared from the scene. Consideration of the other classic dualisms is in a state of quiescence. The place they once held is now filled—as far as not empty—by refining and polishing tools to be used, as far as appears, only in refining more tools of precisely the same kind. For these investigations avowedly are concerned with questions said to be those of form and of form only; that is, not forms of *any* subject matter. This course leads to philosophy's becoming a form of "busy-work" for a few professionals. Otherwise, discussions seem to go into refinements of the history of bygone issues.

Meanwhile there *are* issues of utmost importance. They are indeed so urgent that their importance may be one source of taking refuge in formal issues as an escape. But in any case they are issues marked by that inclusive and underlying character that answers the claim made by traditional philosophy for depth and comprehensiveness as its distinctive mark. The problems concerned with the present state of man in the world are certainly inclusive in range. They are no longer local; they are of man throughout the whole wide world—north, south, east, west. This fact is too obvious to need more than mention. Their temporal range may need more specific attention. The present troubles of man and the resources available for dealing with them lie far back in the abyss of time. Both our means of intercommunication and the barriers that obstruct free exchange of ideas as well as of goods come from pre-human geological ages. More recent but still very ancient is man's animal ancestry. The organism's brain and nerves, as well as stomach and muscles, are the means through which all transactions with nature and with fellow men are carried on. They are also of pre-human origin. The animal is so deep in man *as* man that it is the occasion of many of the abiding troubles of human life.

Yet till recently there has been no basis for placing these troubles in a factual context. Hence there has been no basis for their scientific analysis and statement. Theological ethics has attributed them to the corruption of man in consequence of original sin—demanding therefore the kind of remedy that only a supernatural agency can supply. The prevalent view among moralists not openly accepting the supernatural account attributes the ills in question to the inherent opposition and conflict in human nature between impulse and appetite on one side and reason and will on the other side—all being treated as entitative "faculties," and hence to be dealt with by means that, to say the least, are *extra*-scientific. Of late, psychiatry has developed treatments which come closer than any other devices to being scientific. But it operates in terms which are quasi-mystical. Unconsciousness is set up as an entity—a direct heritage from the earlier attitude that treated "consciousness" as an entity. Recognition that the troubles in question proceed from conflicts between primitive animal elements and the elements that have been shaped by acculturation (i.e., transformed by "social" institutions) renders scientific resources available for specific factual analyses and reports. Their treatment can now be brought into line with the transformation already made in medical treatment of ills by means of use of the methods and conclusions of physical and physiological inquiry.

The foregoing has a certain importance on its own account. It is here mentioned, however, as an illustration. The fact exemplified is, negatively, that the earlier period of modern natural inquiry was such as to evoke and justify the dualisms that were the staples of philosophical discussion; positively, it stands for the fact that natural science in its own advance to maturity now renders these dualisms as unnecessary as they have proved to be futile. The substitution of continuities in the place of breaks and isolations has broken down the separation and opposition of philosophy to natural science—a separation which was inevitable as long as the state of scientific inquiry was definitely adverse to specifically human activities and values. The substitution of extensive continuities for sharp division and isolations has for its foundation the systematic, thoroughgoing abandonment of the frame of reference, the standpoint and outlook, that was the necessary result of the assumption that knowing and knowledge were assured and secure only as they dealt with what is inherently fixed, immutable. When *process* is seen to be the "universal" in nature and in life, continuity, extensive spatially and temporally, becomes *the* regulative principle of *all* inquiry that claims to be scientific.

The change is so recent that it is still generally regarded as technical and confined. It is out of the question to do more here than mention some of the outstanding aspects of that change in the frame of reference of natural inquiry which is anything but technical— which in fact is so extensive as now to render scientific conclusions directly available in and for philosophical inquiry.

Replacement of fixity and the separations consequent upon it by process and continuity was first achieved in the knowing of plant and animal life. For a time, it was incomplete with respect to this subject matter. The category of fixation which was abandoned with respect to "species" was retained in search for immutables in the process of "evolution." More important, of course, was resistance from vested institutional interests, since life—especially human life —was to them the last ditch of entrenched external authority. The persistence of this resistance is now an important—probably *the* most important—factor in maintaining "social" and moral subjects in their notably backward estate.

The objection is made that the inclusion of man and his concerns and values within the scope of continuous process involves degradation of man to the level of the brutes. It comes with particularly poor grace from those who insist upon man's total corruption because of original sin. But it also involves *denial* of continuity of process. For continuity involves variation and differentiation of a cumulative sort, while the doctrine of reductive degradation treats continuity of development as if it were bare repetition. Employment of motion as a basic principle in physics was also partial in its earlier phase. For it was accompanied by the belief that motions occur within a fixed empty shell of space and time, and that they center in and are conducted by immutable atomic particles. Now that the Newtonian framework is replaced by that of relativity (from the standpoint of popular understanding not a very happy name), the old separations of space and time from each other, and of both of them from the events taking place within them, have lost all shadow of standing. Space and time, instead of being nouns or names of "entities," are now qualifications of events, more accurately represented by adverbial form than even by adjectival phrases. "Matter" is represented by a mathematical expression which, like all such symbols, is transformable at need into symbols applicable to other aspects of the indefinitely extensive process which is nature. The "mechanistic" in its earlier sense is now inapplicable save to selected segments and sections which are usable as mechanisms of chosen operations. In the advance alike of physical and physiological inquiry, the fixed separations set up between man and nature make way for specifically determined continuities. The methods and findings of natural science in consequence become available resources for systematic use by philosophic inquiry—provided the latter is willing to make a renunciation that is a sacrifice only for those having vested institutional interests in perpetuating the eternal and immutable as the proper and only assured marks of "Reality" at large as *the* "Object" of science.

In spite of attendant handicaps, the earlier phase of "modern" philosophy made notable contributions to the advancement of the new astronomy and physics. It accomplished this work both negatively and positively. It brought critical attacks to bear upon institutional obstacles that stood in the way—thereby forwarding, whether it was so intended or not, "liberal" movements in the broader human field. They opened up large and generous vistas of the natural world; and projection of these views contributed largely to formation of the specific working instruments that were needed by the new natural science. The heaviest handicap under which philosophy labored in doing this work of liberation was that, instead of doing its work openly, it operated under cover of that which it continued to view as Ultimate Being or Reality at large. Because its work was done under cover, those who engaged in development of the "modern" philosophy of that period mostly failed to note that the service which was genuinely rendered was that of liberation in *human* affairs. In respect to Reality only futile contention resulted. And the service actually rendered was distorted by the assumption that the human in question was isolated from the world with which physical science dealt. The persistent hold of the assumption is best shown in the fact that it was maintained in full force at the very time natural inquiry was actually transforming human relations.

III

Philosophy that is thoroughgoing in acknowledgment that human activities, affairs, successes and failures, trials and tribulations, resources and liabilities, values positive and negative, are its proper subject matter is now able to employ the methods and conclusions of natural inquiry as its systematic ally in performance of its own office: that of furthering observations of the problems that are deeply and widely involved in the contemporary state of man; and that of contributing to formation of a frame of reference in which pertinent hypotheses for dealing with the problems can be projected.

The postulate underlying the validity of this position is, of course, that inquiries in the human field, in the so-called "social" sciences, are now in as backward a state as was physical inquiry a few centuries ago—only "more so." To me this is a fact so obvious that no argument for it is needed. But a few outstanding considerations will be set forth. At present we are not even aware of what the *problems* are in and of the human field. On the overt, so-called "practical" side, the ever-accelerating rate at which the troubles and evils, as the raw materials of problems, are piling up and spreading offers a convincing demonstration of backwardness. Further evidence is furnished by two significant features of the attitude taken toward them. One is the current revival of the policy of despair embodied in the doctrine that man's sinful nature is the source of these troubles so that recourse to the supernatural is indicated—the former optimistic assumption that exhortation and idealistic preaching will suffice being now pretty effectively discounted.

The other feature is the policy of despair represented in the current clamor of accusations that natural science is itself a chief source of a large number of present evils, and that arresting its further development (instead of use in constructive advancement of competent human inquiry) is the remedy to be employed. Evidence of backwardness on what is usually called the "theoretical" side (as if it were not itself supremely practical) is equally convincing. It is not excessive to say that at present social maladjustments and ills are taken "as is"—in the raw, as if they were of themselves problems in the scientific sense. This is precisely as if in physics the destruction of houses by lightning, or the harmful deterioration of metal by rusting, were taken not as the occasion of search for the conditions that constitute the problem, but as itself the problem; or as if in physiology the occurrence of malaria and of cancer were taken in their brute occurrence to be scientific problems. In the case of "lightning," it is clear that no scientific progress was made until it was at least determined where the problem was located— namely, in the field of electrical events—and that further progress in specific determination of the problem occurred as physics progressed in understanding of electrical phenomena. Until malaria was located in the general field of infection by parasites of insect origin, attempts to deal with it were purely "empirical" in the disparaging sense of that word. The case of cancer is even more significant. In short, the saying that problems well stated are already half solved errs only in not going far enough. Problem-stating and problem-solving are two aspects of one and the same operation. It is because of this fact that the present state of "problems" in the subject matter of human inquiry is so deplorably significant.

Further evidence as to the backward state of inquiry in this field is the assumption that now possesses pretty complete control of inquiry into human subject matter. This assumption is that the

various important aspects of organized human behavior are so isolated from one another as to constitute separate and independent
subjects, and hence are to be treated each one by methods peculiar
to it in its severalty. The subject matter is chopped up and parceled out into, say, jurisprudence, politics, economics, the fine arts,
religion, and morals. "Sociology" in its origin was presented as a
means of overcoming this splitting up; it seems to have developed
into another subject with its own special subject matter—which it
has been largely occupied with attempting to determine. In this connection, it is profitable to note that physical inquiry in its earlier
phase was also divided into separate subjects; and that its progress
is marked by inquiries that have to be designated by introducing
hyphens and adjectival phrases. The distinction among them is fast
becoming one of phase or emphasis in the direction of inquiry, not
one of barriers due to the subject matters.

What has been said will be misunderstood if it is taken to signify that philosophy can or should offer solutions for human problems or even determine on its own account what the problems
specifically are. But there is a preliminary work urgently in need
of doing. It is similar to that done in the seventeenth, eighteenth,
and a large part of the nineteenth centuries in getting physical inquiry free from the burdens that were imposed by cultural conditions of earlier periods; and, positively, in building up a sense of
the frame of reference, the kind of standpoint and of outlook, in
which human problems are to be specified, and hypotheses for their
resolution projected and tested. It is worth while to note again that
human subject matter now has spatially and temporally the comprehensive scope that philosophic reflection has claimed as its own
distinguishing mark. The breakdown of the barriers between man
and nature now extends so far and wide that the futile problem of
the dualism of mind-and-body may be exchanged for specific problems as to how transactions of organism and environment as they
take place retard and assist human endeavors for humane ends.
The question of "natural resources" is much less confined than is
usually supposed; it needs broadening to take in the way in which

natural conditions enter into every phase of human concern, whether as resource or as liability.

What was just said about the inclusive and penetrating state of human activities and concerns indicates that one of the prime problems today is to show that human material in its full scope is now the proper subject matter of philosophy. The case of assaults upon "science" as if it were an entity by itself, having its own independent career, is a case in point—as is equally the indiscriminate laudations sometimes lavished upon it. What is called science, like knowing in every form, is one aspect of organized human behavior; it is so far from being isolated and independent that it is engaged in and shaped by continual transactions of give-and-take with every other form of organized human behavior. There is an open field awaiting students of the historical aspects of philosophy in showing how the course of natural science has been affected by the cultural concerns in religious rites and dogmas, in economics, politics, law, and the arts, whether "fine" or "useful." What is wanted is not a "synthesis," a formal unification imposed from without, but specific studies of intercommunication, and of the blocks and arrests that have unduly exaggerated one phase of human behavior and minimized other phases—as, for one example, the historic cultural conditions which rendered physical inquiry so one-sidedly specialized as to give it its present predominatingly technical temper. Systematic pursuit of this line of inquiry will remove morals from the narrow isolated field in which it has been progressively confined by disclosing the demonstrable fact that it is the culmination and focus of what is distinctively humane in all values and disvalues of all the modes and aspects of collective, organized behavior.

The way ahead is hard and difficult for philosophy as for every other phase of human endeavor; for, after all, the change demanded in philosophy is but one aspect of the reconstructions now possible and urgently required in every phase of human life. Philosophy can hardly take the lead in introducing that new epoch in human history which is now the alternative to ever-increasing catastrophe. But it can, if it has enduring courage and patience, engage cooperatively in the prolonged struggle to discover and utilize the positive ways and means by which the cause of human freedom and justice may be advanced in spite of the uncertainties, confusions, and active conflicts that now imperil civilization itself. The opportunity for engaging in co-operative work is open. The initial step in philosophical endeavor is systematic, constructive use of the resources that the different phases of natural inquiry have now put in our hands. Utilization *in fact* of these resources must of course extend far beyond the particular activities called by the names of either science or philosophy. But those engaged in philosophical pursuits can, if they will, have a share in the undertaking, thereby regaining for the subject to which they have pledged themselves significance and vitality which are generous, liberal, humane.

It may well be that the isolation of "science" from other organized human pursuits, occupations, and values was originally a measure of protection. Perhaps if it had not disclaimed responsibility for connection with and bearing upon other aspects of collective activity and concern, the institutional obstacles to its survival would have been more than grave; they might have been insuperable. But nonetheless acceptance of the doctrine of its systematic aloofness left its course to be one-sidedly determined by and connected with one particular type of human interest and behavior —that termed Economic which in turn was identified with the "material." This identification and the isolations that followed in consequence have conferred undue strength upon institutional operations that have tended to enhance the profit and power of class sections and nationalistic segments at the expense of our common humanity. This state of human life inevitably recoils to produce insecurity and conflict. A choice of immense human import will be made in the coming days. We shall either perpetuate and intensify the evils that tragically afflict us by continuing petulant and futile complaints directed at natural inquiry, or we shall begin to utilize the physical, intellectual, and moral resources provided by scientific understanding to promote conditions of freedom, equity, and well-being in which all human beings share. The choice reaches so deep and wide that the career and destiny of philosophy is but one factor among many. But for philosophy its part is not minor. It now has the opportunity and challenge to take part by showing how systematic use of the resources provided by the methods and conclusions of natural inquiry can serve the interests of our common humanity. Philosophy that assumes a responsible even if humble share in this work will drink of living springs from which to draw renewed vitality.

3

Of Truth

HORACE M. KALLEN

Professor, New School for Social Research

FOR SPEECH TO BE FREE, Max Otto points out in a new attack upon the problem of that freedom,[1] there must be the right and power to listen as well as the power and right to talk. So long as speech is only soliloquy, no problem of its freedom need arise. Issues are raised when speech is communication, and freedom of speech is far more a function of freedom to listen than freedom to talk. A world where speech is really free would be a world of human beings educated in the arts, and equipped with the spiritual and material means, of listening. To construct such a world,

. . . the search for truth must capture the imagination of men as an exciting experience, and a preference for the sharpest truth-tools must be made the rule instead of the exception. An idealism having its root and flower and fruit in the occupations of every day, elevating the ends which are sought in making a living as in making a life, must replace super-earthly idealism. Men must learn to distrust the primitive and deceptive glamor of fighting it out and grow up to the mature art of conferring with each other for the purpose of extracting a mutually appealing mode of conduct from conflicting and incompatible interests.

Society thus conceived implies profound changes in current habits and

---

[1] "Speech and Freedom of Speech," in *Freedom and Experience*, edited by Sidney Hook and Milton R. Konvitz (Ithaca and New York: Cornell University Press, 1947).

current beliefs. These changes will be strenuously resisted by at least two powerful groups, each of which at bottom assumes the depravity of human nature—the one by acting on the theory that man is inherently a materialistic, self-seeking creature, the other by exploiting man's proneness to superstitious ideas in the absence of authentic knowledge. Any compromise with the working principle of either of these groups is in my judgment a flagrant betrayal of mankind.

II

No one can fail to be moved by these words, so wise, so brave, and so eloquent. They envision afresh the conditions as well as the springs of a good most desirable and excellent, and propose that free men shall establish and make secure that good. Like all philosophical proposals, they have their contexts. One is the belief that truth is not possessed but still to seek among the generality of mankind. Another is that those for whom it is to seek know what they are looking for. Still another is that the seekers are sure what tools to use, and by what means to keep them at their sharpest. There is also the assumption, as generous as it is bold, that men can at one and the same time attain a reconciliation of conflicting and incompatible interests and refuse all compromise with the working principle of certain of such interests. They communicate a confidence which takes me back to a time in my youth when, for a certain circle of philosophers, practically all assumptions regarding the nature of truth had been once more jolted out of their places in the structure of settled belief and promoted to the status of controversial issues. The philosophic enterprise was then a battle over living, forced, and momentous options between answers to the question "What is truth?" The heroes and giants debated; James and Dewey talked of the human mind, and Bradley and Royce of God's. So far as I can remember almost everybody retired from the field victorious, one or another perhaps convinced against his will but of the same opinion still. John Russell, I think, did come round to James's view regarding the nature of truth, and Bertrand Russell, long after the controversy had subsided, almost persuaded himself: his basic beliefs had, however, been fixed too soon and

too firmly not to settle back upon their old foundations.[2] On the
whole and in the long run, the argument came to no consensus.
The debate died away without concluding. The philosophic denominations simply turned to other interests. But they continue

---

[2] I am impelled to add that, as I read Russell these days, the struggle seems not
simply to have left scars, but to have quieted down to a kind of cold war in his
psyche. His more recent utterances, especially the last one about "the impact of
science on society," seem to me often to be venting the sort of aggression that
psychoanalysts are known to attribute to struggle with ambivalence. I cannot see that
the logic of this argument regarding what science is doing to and for society called for
any animadversions on Dewey and pragmatism at all. Russell seems to have gone out
of his way to make the ideas of the pragmatists over into something that is to him
altogether no good. He charges pragmatists with reducing truth to utility by putting
what is useful in the place of what is so—as if usefulness, even as an inalterable
essence, could be usefulness of nothing at all instead of a process by which something gets changed to something else. By means of this charge, Russell is able to
rationalize his degrading pragmatism into a "police theory of truth" and a power
philosophy which puts truth to "the arbitrament of the big battalions," and able
to do so in the name of the very freedom of which, he, more than anybody, should
know pragmatists to be the champions and vindicators.

I cannot help seeing in this particular translation of pragmatic thought something
malicious and unworthy. For I cannot see how, save on the score of suppression
into unconsciousness, Russell can fail to be aware of the long history of John Dewey
and other pragmatists as unyielding champions of freedom in every field where
the pursuit of knowledge and the formation of belief signify. How, without such
suppression, could he fail to be aware that the pragmatic movement—which breathes
the very spirit of liberalism, treating logic as a method of inquiry and not a
metaphysic of existence, treating all principles, religious as well as scientific, not as
infallible revelation, but as working hypotheses, looking to consequences not
guaranteed in advance—is a critical phase of the modern struggle for civil and
intellectual liberty? How, without such suppression, could he fail to be aware that
its findings concerning the nature of truth are a critical moment in this struggle?
That the pragmatist reports regarding truth's origins, development, relationships,
and functions are libertarian consequences of this struggle?

Even if his skeptical lordship's metaphysical prejudices be in fact the infallible
principles he employs them as, neither his descriptions of, nor his inferences regarding, pragmatist theories of truth could follow from the theories themselves. At
most, the diverse and diversifying actualities of experience, belief, and knowledge
which the theories bespeak would continue to flow, unarrested and uncontaminated
by the One, Eternal, Universal Truth of his lordship's worship, standing absolute
and without relation to any actuality which our minds do apprehend and understand,
yet invoked to condemn whatever varies. For, on the record, authoritarian practices
and infallibilist pretensions have gone, at least since Plato, with the species of Truth
that Russell as epistemologist exalts and as citizen disregards. In so far as he preaches
and practices intellectual freedom, he denies the authoritarian, necessary Truth which
is his lord. In so far as he affirms this transcendental Truth, he plays it false by his
stand for free thought, against authoritarian tyrannies of every sort. His practices

to cherish their numerous diverse and conflicting beliefs concerning the nature of truth with an assurance that the great debate seems in no way to have diminished.

These denominations are too many to count up here. They keep dividing and combining, forming and re-forming into varieties and subvarieties of idealists, realists, materialists, and pragmatists; naturalists, supernaturalists and neutralists; monists, dualists, and pluralists; logical positivists, phenomenologists, and epi-phenomenalists; neo-Hegelians of the left and of the right, neo-Thomists of the right and of the center; existentialists of the left and existentialists of the right, absolutists and relativists, eternalists, and temporalists, and so on forever. The combinations and permutations continue with no *terminus ad quem,* and each brings along its own singular truth-tool by which to cut truth loose from error. Unless a truth-seeker jests like Bacon's Pilate—asking, "What is truth?" and not staying for an answer—he finds himself confronted, if his curiosity persists, with a variety of answers to choose from. No ratiocination or rationalization, not even the solipsistic kind, can relieve him of the hazards of choosing.

These hazards, I gather, are intrinsic to the experience of a genuine truth-seeking. This seeking does not start in a vacuum. It stars from a complex of beliefs already held. Let the components of this complex be imposed from without, or let them be personal

---

seem more loyal to the logic of freedom than his epistemological preachment. He seems to want his necessitarian principles with their authoritarian implications to come to an harmonious fulfillment in his libertarian practices with their contingent conclusions.

The tone and manner of his current denigration of pragmatist attitudes and thought testify, I think, to a psychological predicament even more than to a logical impasse. The attraction which pragmatism has for Russell is now perhaps quite unconscious. But it is nonetheless dynamic in his thinking and expression, and his resistance to it emerges in his ways of talking about Dewey and his assaults on pragmatism as a "police theory of truth," "power-philosophy," and the like. On the record, he knows better and knows that he knows better. Epistemologically, he has become a St. Anthony among logisticians, withdrawn to the desert of noetic absolutism, half embracing and half repelling the pragmatist perspectives which guide his stand for freedom, and which he consequently curses as works of the devil of totalitarian authoritarianism, which is his own logistical *deus absconditus.*

choices—if the seeker were content with them, truth would be his possession and not his desire. Searching and seeking follow discontent with the already possessed. Whichever one of its multitudinous springs the discontent flows from, it begins as uncertainty regarding the already possessed, moves to challenge and denial of it, develops as alienation from it, and terminates in its complete repudiation. By complete repudiation a true belief has been reappraised into a false belief. Not uncommonly the repudiation of one belief is concurrent with the adoption of another, the seeker taking this other for his true belief. But the concurrence is not necessary. A mind may decide that a belief it had held for true has become false without replacing it by a different one—just as a spouse may divorce a spouse without there being another woman or man in the case.

One hazard of the option turns on the usually ignored contingency that it is a social event. Even for the philosophical solipsist the decision is not soliloquy but communication. Creations of his belief as his fellow debaters may dialectially be, he perforce addresses his creatures as his peers, and their responses involve consequences that control him and that he can only struggle to control. And this was as valid of alone-living Robinson Crusoe as of any solipsistic professor of philosophy. The ways of experimental science are here no guide. Alike the import and the importance of a belief alter with time and place and circumstance. If, in Lilliput, which end is the right end to open an egg causes a civil war, in Europe men have fought through generations bloodily over such propositions as that something which looks like bread and feels like bread and tastes like bread is really flesh and blood. The propositions which currently engage their fighting faith may be held in similar esteem. There is no belief that somebody does not exalt into a fighting faith. To affirm as true a belief which makes falsehoods of cherished beliefs of one's neighbors, one's profession, one's communion, one's entire world—to declare a belief false which to one's fellows is the very depth and height of truth—remains still among the multitudes of the earth a hazard of hatred and slander, of torture, war, and destruction.

Yet the *what* of a belief is neutral to the judgment of its truth; the issue is its *how*. During the great debate, the options between truths about truth did not seem to turn much on "the state of the case" or the cogency of the arguments. By and large the dispute seemed only to heighten each disputant's conviction of the indisputable rightness of his denomination's image of truth, and he figured as an honored champion in the stronghold of his sect. In effect, each tended to argue a foregone conclusion, and his argument was far more a display of dialectical prowess than an inquiry into the truth about truth. Addressed to the philosophical elect, it left out of its conspectus all sorts of beliefs that plain men hold as truths to live by, everywhere in the world. Instead of inquiring into the *how* of their trueness, some brethren of the craft condemned them as "vital lies," others as "superstitions," others as "willful errors," or heresies. Truth was appraised by this or that minority as its own special privileged possession, while the diverse truths of the residual minorities who together make up the great majority became automatically errors, perhaps fraught with death.

And this is the continuing state of affairs. This is the tradition and the custom. Turn to what part of the human scene you like, you will find perceptions and ideas which some minds hold for true and others simultaneously for false; which confront some with critical options calling for total assent or total rejection, while remaining completely indifferent to others. The history of the arts and sciences provides a similar experience. It is replete with ideas that had been held for true and discarded as false, and others that had been held for false, or ignored, and been adopted for true. The same idea, it would seem on the record, may be both true and false at the same time to different minds, or true at one time and false at another to the same mind. In the circumstances, "truth" and "error" can hardly be taken to name inward properties of the existences they qualify, let these existences be what they may. They are terms of external relation, not substance, designating traits adjoined and not traits essential and constitutive.

I have nothing to add to the account I choose from among the available alternative accounts of what these traits are. James has

said it, Dewey has said it, Schiller has said it, Mead has said it. I
have also had my own say on other occasions. At this time I can
only write a gloss upon the earlier deliverances.

That which translates an experience from an event or datum into
a truth or an error is the way a mind takes, thinks, uses it. As it
enter a stream of consciousness it is simply a passing given. It goes
on, it goes out, and it has made no difference. If, however, attention pick it up out of the multitudinous flow, fix on it, hold it,
strive to get ever closer to it, then it is making a difference. It has
become an interest, and the man's actions with respect to it establish it as an object of his belief. We believe in those entries into our
experience that we *have liefer*—that is, prefer to others. And we
prefer those which in one way or many continue to sustain and
strengthen the activity of preferring. *Believe* and *belove* grow, if the
dictionaries are to be trusted, from the same root. They name the
attitudes and actions, at times indescribably diversified and complex,
by which something on the move is slowed up, held back, sustained, confirmed, enhanced. Believing and beloving establish what
is initially far and strange as near and dear. They designate ways
of living with persons, with things, with ideas. The words *true* and
false come in when we pass from a certain state of believing or loving to a later phase. A man's "true love" is no automatic sweetheart, but one whose behavior so cherishes and strengthens her
lover's love that it diversifies and grows; love is false which fails
of such consequences. Truth here involves be-*troth*al, private or
public or both, and betrothal is a relation such that each lover
troweth the other with a trust whose validity for each is its consequences to his love. The consequences are eventualities, not foregone conclusions; it is well known, even among the infallible, that
there are times when a true love does become a false one. The relationship is such that a personality first strange and indifferent has
become familiar, precious, and reassuring, its existence necessary
thus, and thereby rational; its survival and growth have ceased to
be mere events but have been made into signs of something other
than themselves—namely, the lover's love and welfare. In the lan-

guage of the profession, what started as knowledge-of-acquaintance has been enlarged into knowledge-about. This enlargement is its "meaning," by virtue of which it is now true or false.

So also with beliefs. Whatever their contents, they come first as knowledge-of-acquaintance. When a believer employs them to mean an experience other than themselves, when he makes of them signs or symbols, thus endowing them with meaning, he establishes them as knowledge-about. They are then to him predicates, pointers, directed toward a meant, leading closer to it, coming next to it, and at long last perhaps so consummating themselves in it that the meaning and the meant are no longer two but one. Even as a past event, a meant is a future experience. But the idea or image or symbol or percept which means it is no empty process of recovery. It is a forward-going activity of approximation and identification, thus of alteration. The mere self-repetition of an identical, if it be operative, alters it. Moreover, the contents of beliefs are of many kinds and are continually reappraised and reclassified in many and diversifying ways, among them the hardy perennials called appearance and reality, fact and fiction. These pairs the tradition holds of prime importance to the determination of truth and error. As "true" believers make use of them, however, they function as categories of value rather than existence. Let the attributed origin of any event be whatever you choose, it enters experience the equal of every other. Its appraisal as reality or appearance, as fact or fiction, follows not from what it is just known as, but from what the believer does with it. From his doings an equation comes which renders truth the same as reality or fact, error or falsehood the same as fiction or appearance. What has started as duality or plurality has been assimilated into unity, and the true and the real, the idea and its object, have been fused into identity. Error, on the other hand, is left without an object. And except for absolute idealists whose theory of truth makes it the synthesis of all the errors, an error, if it be still error, hangs loose, a miracle of non-existent existence.

Epistemologists, logicians, and metaphysicians, endeavoring to give stability and consistency to these strange events, sometimes identify the triads, treating each pair as if its signs were interchangeable synonyms, as in the theologian's Trinity. At other times the dialectical imagination will declare the triads parallels that never meet and affirm an unaltering and inalterable correspondence between truth and reality and truth and fact. Sometimes it will admit or declare that the postulated reality to which truth corresponds is a thing outside any actual experience, present or to come, an inexperienceable "thing-in-itself." There are those who list among such inexperienceables both the past we remember and the past we do not remember. Knowing them truly, they then tell us, requires that an idea of them should hold in a coherent system of relations. But when you try to bring their meanings up to something specifically meant, you find that all they have for you is a sign of a sign of a sign of a sign, on and on, to the day they die generated and sustained by their own activity as believers. In other words, those transcendent terms and relations are the believers' postulates. If they are the thing he hopes for, their substance is only his belief. If they are the things not seen, his belief is their only evidence.

In the course of time, the accumulation and organization of signs and symbols actually experienceable, which are consequences of his belief, will compose a weighty body of support for this belief. It will be an institution such as a church or a state or a legal system or an economic establishment, each with its "body of knowledge." The life of man creates many such institutions and is spent among them from birth to death. The world that even the simplest and most naïve human being lives most intimately in is a world of signs and symbols, a world of meanings by faith created and by generations of faith transmitted, altered, and maintained. He lives on credit, and, if he cashes in, the promissory notes are all there is to take with him. Let his belief falter or fail, and the substance dissipates to shadow and the evidence to error.

These things considered, the sense in which seeing is believing is far from always sensory. Experience often finds that believing is seeing. The Vermont farmer who proclaimed, when he first inspected a camel, "Pshaw! There ain't no such animal!" exemplifies this finding no less than the churchmen who jailed, starved, tortured, and burned alive persons who affirmed that the sun stands still and the earth moves, in face of the fact that daily men's eyes confirmed what God's word revealed and earthly authority upheld, that the earth stands still and the sun moves. To this day we do see the sun rise and set. Nor has higher criticism altered the deliverances of the Bible which confirm our senses; nor, so far as I know, have God's infallible vicegerents ever rescinded their condemnation of the belief that "the sun is the centre about which the earth revolves." As Andrew D. White tells the story in the third chapter of the first volume of his *History of the Warfare of Science with Theology in Christendom,* a signed and sealed papal bull, *Speculatores domus Israel,* was in 1664, attached to the Vatican's *Index of Forbidden Books.* The purpose of the bull, says White, was to bind the contents upon the faithful; to confirm and approve expressly, finally, decisively, infallibly, the condemnation of "all books teaching the movements of the earth and the stability of the sun." On the record, the infallible authority of the Divine Son's infallible vicar continues to stand pledged in principle to the belief that the fundamental propositions of today's astronomy regarding the solar system are false, and the pre-Copernican propositions true. We have here a confrontation of seeing as believing and believing as seeing. If, since 1664, the latter has displaced the former even in the sanctums of the Deity's infallible spokesmen themselves, there are other domains of belief where the options are reversed. For example, the late Heywood Broun, in taking the dogmas of the Roman Catholic scheme of salvation for true, took for true such propositions concerning cosmic topography as the existence of the locus and uses of Purgatory. He could do this only if believing were seeing. Conversions from Catholic to Communist dogmas, or Communist to Catholic, and back again, are choices between alternatives which involve believing as seeing, and making truth into error and error into truth.

Similarly, if any honest and sincere men or women took the Hitlerite *Weltanschauung* for true, they could not but regard the deliverances on non-Nazi physics, astronomy, and anthropology as false; the observations of Franz Boas would look to them as heretical and corrupt as the calculations of Albert Einstein. Honest and sincere men or women who believe that Lenin's *Weltanschauung* as amended by Stalin is true will see those of our own social scientists, historians, artists, musicians, physicists, and biologists as false. Recently, the Communist Inquisition has focused on the experiments and findings of non-Communist geneticists. It condemns them as false. In believing Soviet Russia, Mendel, Morgan, and Bateson are the fathers of lies; the Mendelian theory is the priestly invention of a capitalist fantasy, bringing false proof that the bourgeois are the innately superior. But the Lenino-Stalinist truth is that acquired characteristics are inheritable—that if you improve environments you change bad stock into good without benefit of genes, chromosomes, and the rest of the paraphernalia of modern genetics. T. D. Lysenko has done so, changing the nature of tomatoes, wheat, rye, potatoes, thus. He is the prophet of Communist biology. One Russian biologist, L. Vavilov, who held that genetic science as non-Russians know it is true, was sentenced to a concentration camp, where he died. Another, A. R. Zherbak, who urged that Soviet science was not different from science as men of science elsewhere practiced it, and who looked askance at Lysenko, was charged with heresy and removed from his presidency of the White Russian Academy of the Sciences. Once more, believing shaped seeing, making truth of error and error of truth.

III

If, however, the reliability of a belief is appraised not by its immediate *what,* but by its consequential *how,* attention shifts from the orthodoxy of the believer to the processes by which the preferred idea sustains itself by its own powers on its own merits, through the consequences it generates among the events to which it refers.

The truly modern mind is signalized by this shift of attention, and the consequent reappraisal of the nature of truth. These underlie what is esteemed as "scientific method." A critical example of their operation is the new way of appraising the idea that man is an immortal soul lodging in a mortal body, and that, hence, when the body dies the soul continues to live on in such places as Limbo, Purgatory, Hell, or Heaven (where recently also the body of God's Mother has been domiciled by infallible declaration of God's earthly vicar).

There are, in addition, all the other topographical doctrines and behavioral disciplines which have been cultivated from this seed. There is the entire aggregation of beliefs that ecclesiastical interests affirmed and that scientists refused to investigate by the methods of science. All of them can be logically referred to the ineffable dogma that men are alive when they are dead. Long ago William James, recognizing that a belief confirmed by the method of science acquires a reliability lacking in those not so confirmed, challenged the exclusion from scientific inquiry of the belief in an immortal soul separate and distinct from the mortal body. He held the exclusion to be based upon a dogmatism as narrow, as prejudiced, as unscientific as any orthodox theologian's. Without immortality, Limbo, Purgatory, Hell, and Heaven fall from the status of ineffable realities to that of poetic landscapes. With immortality, they are loci of space and time, and fields of destiny with reference to which men frame their rules of life. Yet in the experience of any actual lifetime they figure only as poetic landscapes, images, symbols, and so do the souls assumed to dwell in them. They are all believed in, not seen. Their substantial difference from nature and experience is always an inference, never an observation. And the stuff of the inference is always an emotion, an image, a ritual in use by a church or a temple and its hierophants, employing their powers, their functions, and their words, words, words. The scientific validation of their total meaning could take place only as the scientific validation of any other meaning takes place— through the employment of experiment, calculation, statistical and other measurement, prediction, and whatever else is available to check belief for reliability.

This was the intent of such voluntary groups as the European and American Societies for Psychical Research. Later, psychological laboratories in institutions of higher learning took over the enterprise and labored to give it the cachet of academic regularity. They employed experimentation and statistics as major techniques in confirming or shaking trust in the idea that people are alive when they are dead. They brought into being a new discipline with a new "scientific" dialect—"parapsychology," which made inquiries into telepathy, clairvoyance, precognition, and psychokinesis. These words name powers that a person is assumed by some to exercise only if he is a soul independent of his body. The reliability of the assumption was made a function of the satisfactoriness of the methods of testing, counting, and verifying the practices and their consequences, which go by these names. Satisfactoriness would transvalue assumption into inference.

This shift from *what* to *how* turned the idea of immortality from an ineffable dogma into the scientific problem. It took attention from a perhaps passionately preferred *what* to a consequential *how* in whose scrutiny the power of preference was to be as neutralized as might be. Now, it is the acceptance or rejection of the *how* that makes error into truth or truth into error. Challenge or denial is not condemned or punished as heresy but acknowledged, even welcomed, as test. To meet it, measurement and experiment are repeated or modified; believers cheerfully undertake by their means to resolve the doubts and dissolve the objections of the opponents. The result sought is to render the consequential evidence of the preferred idea—which *is* its truth—more evident and more trustworthy.[3] That is, the techniques commonly recognized as the method of science are employed to convert seeing as an exclusive

---

[3] See William James, "Report on Mrs. Piper's Hodgson Control," in *The Proceedings of the British Society for Psychical Research,* Vol. LVIII (1909); Dunn, *An Experiment with Time;* J. B. Rhine, *New Frontiers of the Mind* and *The Reach of the Mind;* René Warcollier, *Mind to Mind.*

effect of believing into seeing as a vision of events not dependent on believing. The truth of the idea of immortality is no longer taken to derive from a believing which generates the seeing and is referred to a seeing which generates the believing. The reference still turns on an act of choice by the believer, and telepathic and other events can be and are still attributed to other causes than immortal souls. The opposed believers need, however, no longer war with one another over the *what* of belief; they join their forces in improving the *how* which should support the *what,* thereby making truth into error and error into truth.

Indeed, on the record, not only the cults of religion but also the free sciences of man and of nature are such continual reshapings of the substance of things hoped for, and the evidences of things not seen. They begin in beliefs which are decisions between alternatives. These beliefs, however immediately gratifying, are nevertheless not taken as inalterable revelations, self-evident, universal, infallible, therefore exempt from doubt, taboo to inquiry and proof. The scientific believer is distinguished from other kinds in that he enters his beliefs as competitors in a field, without privilege, without favor, and without fear. He enters them claiming that they can do the same job better than their competitors, and he asks for the opportunity to put them to work on equal terms with their competitors, the opportunity to try them out by means of discussion, computation, dialectical analysis, laboratory experiment, the works and ways of daily life, and whatever else might test the meaning of his beliefs. Ideas, preferred and chosen though they be, he is not likely to call beliefs. His words for them will be assumption, postulate, construct, working hypothesis, theory. If their workings consummate their meaning satisfactorily, he may call them laws and ascribe truth to them. Their truth will be an achievement, not an endowment; an acquired characteristic, not an innate trait. To retain their acquisition they will continually work against competing alternatives claimed to do the same job better. They will remain truths so long as no competitor makes good its counter-claim. There will be occasions when the competition will result in a draw, and the affirmation of one belief as against another will revert from warrant by consequence to option by believer. But belief very rarely is held on that level. The believer seeks differentiating consequences. Again and again and again, the accolade of truth does not accrue to a belief from *what* it is, or *where* it comes from, or *who* believes in it. The *what* may be supernaturalist as well as naturalist; the *where* may be a bank, a church, or a chapel as well as a laboratory; the *who* may be the humblest of men as well as the most elect of experts. But the belief's truth will eventually accrue to it from *how it works,* from the consequences that ensue upon its meanings. And should it become false, it will come to its falsehood in the same way.

IV

Neither the history of ideas nor the immediacies of experience warrant the belief that at least some propositions are and must be true not only everywhere and at all times but true eternally and universally. It was Charles Peirce, a believer in truth so qualified, who said somewhere that if man could live forever he could be perfectly sure of seeing the day when everything in which he had trusted should betray his trust, and that he too would break down at last. The need to trust is, however, inveterate in us; and when we can no longer trust, we perish. A synonym for the need to trust is "the will to believe." Believing is trusting, trowing, taking for true and making true. The more and more different human beings believe it together, the more trustworthy his belief feels to the believer, whatever his vocation. Alternatives are usually most unwelcome challenges. They shake his security and break his peace. Only long experience of the advantage which challenge brings to this security can teach him to tolerate alternatives. But for the most part he will try anything from laughter to slaughter to shut out and cut off the unbearable idea.

When he learns at long last to acquiesce in the mutability of all experienced events, he may come to believe (as Mr. Justice Holmes pointed out in the Schenck case), even more than he believes in the very foundations of his own conduct, that the ultimate good desired is better reached by free trade in ideas, that the best test of truth is the power of thought to get itself accepted in the competition of the market; and that truth is the only ground upon which his wishes can be carried out. Then he may compensate for the insecurities he undergoes, because of the mutations of truths into errors and back again amid the changes and chances of his experience, by postulating a final, predestined, inalterable, universal, and eternal Truth which shall guarantee certainty to his heart and repose to his mind. This is the thing hoped for and the thing not seen to which the belief of Charles Peirce lent substance and provided evidence—"the opinion which is fated to be ultimately agreed upon by all who investigate is what we mean by the truth, and the object represented in this opinion is the real." He speaks of it also as the "predestinate opinion," the opinion that "can nohow be avoided" and is "sure to come true." John Dewey, I am curious to note, appraises this hypostasis of the instrument as "the best definition of truth from the logical standpoint." [4]

Over against the many singular truths which some believers trust all of their lifetime and others some of their lifetime, there stands then eternally this one total Truth, still undiscovered, perhaps never to be discovered, which all of the believers must infallibly trust all of their lifetime. This is the Truth which, however crushed to earth, shall rise again, and which science is declared to seek.

For the actualities of the search for truth, for the practice of inquiry, and for the conduct of life, nevertheless, we need not take this compensatory ideal into account. It becomes important to the enterprises of the inquiring intelligence when some society of believers identify their own singular system of doctrines with this fatality of knowledge, and not only cease to search for truth themselves but forcibly end the search by others. Since they already have the truth, why should anybody seek it? Such a search becomes for them a willful pursuit of error, a corruption of morality, a

---

[4] *Logic*, p. 345n.

defiance of authority, loathsome and fraught with death. Should some dissident refuse to concede the claims of this society, asserting for his own preferred belief power to do the same job better than that doctrine enthroned and adored, he may receive such treatment as was given to Kepler, to Campanella, to Giordano Bruno, to Galileo, to Servetus, to Roger Williams, to Spinoza, and to all the inventors and discoverers who brought new thoughts and new ways to mankind.

Of these, some submit and conform; others cling to their beliefs despite the power of the orthodox, the incredulity of the learned, the climate of opinion, and the immense loneliness of their self-isolation. Though they know that their truth will slay them, they trust in it. That it should bring them death is their warrant of its survival-value for them. For their antagonists do not require that they should die; they require that the believers should denounce their truth as error, and all the cruelties they are made to suffer are intended to accomplish this conversion. If, then, the believers had liefer perish than accept another faith, it is they who succeed and their foes who fail. If to the power-holders their truth makes of them criminals deserving the cruel death, to such few as they can persuade they are martyrs to the truth. Though you might not think so, their method has been what Peirce calls "the method of tenacity." He suggests that its users are enviable because they "can dismiss reason," and it is true of course that their opponents often accuse them of just that. On the record, however, they may be employing a method of thought as much a variant from the prevailing conventions of reason as their beliefs are from the truths prevailing. After they are dead they may be celebrated as our age celebrates so many inventors, discoverers, and innovators, including Peirce himself, for the very deviations which cost them their safety, or their freedom, or their lives.

Tenacity is the condition prior to the use of any and all instruments of the truth-seeking intelligence. Consider how few still are the minorities who believe in the method of science, how weak, how dependent; how overwhelmingly large the multitudes to whom those methods are strange, evil, and fraught with death; how power-ful the authorities who rule as custodians and policemen of the dominant faiths among the multitudes. Then ask: How well, how long, could the methods of science survive as working alternatives to those dominations if the men of science were not tenacious of their beliefs and did not hold freedom to seek the truth as a fighting faith which they will never yield?

The issues of error and truth depend for their decision on this precarious freedom—that is, on the *how* of our knowing and not the *what* of our knowledge. That idea cannot be fully trusted whose truth draws for its validation upon consequences not flowing from the idea itself. This was Roger Williams' insight; it was John Milton's fighting faith. Both men were devout Christians. Both held a system of beliefs of whose truth they were certain beyond every doubt. Both had, however, come to see, in those years of the great initiatives of the scientific imagination which was their age, that their certainties must draw from the *how* of their believings, not the *what*. So Williams would admit the right of even atheists to their thought, and Milton exalted "the liberty to know, to utter, and to argue freely according to conscience, above all other liberties." The only thing that its limitation could do, he urged in *Areopagit-ica,* would be to atrophy our powers in the already known, to hobble and dwarf future knowledge, whether religious or secular, "to the discouragement of all learning and the stop of truth." Lacking free inquiry and free discussion, "the waters of truth sicken into a muddy pool of conformity and tradition." Even at that, uni-formity is unattainable, while variety is driven underground, and life is deprived of the condition of its betterment. Liberty is the precondition to the establishment of new truth and the survival of old.

Whatever men may take for true, its truth continues a function of its freedom. Freedom is indispensable, John Mill, in his *Essay on Liberty,* argued. The coercion of thought and expression was to him the worst of coercions. For it makes impossible the elimination of error by truth if the imposed opinion should be wrong, and the clarification of truth "by its collision with error" if the imposed opinion should be right; while the imposing authority must pretend to infallibility. Only in the free competition of the market, where competitors can check each other's merits, can a claim to truth be reliably maintained. In that competition, a false idea can't survive as useful, and the true idea emerges as one which has done its cognitive job better than all its competitors. What alone persecution accomplishes is to make truth scarce and dangerous. Yet martyrdom is no proof of it; men suffer and die for ideas that after they die turn out to be errors. For, intrinsically, true ideas are no more powerful than false ones. Truth, crushed to earth, does not necessarily rise again. Men, knowing this, may endeavor to appease power-holders. They may, like Descartes, disguise what they do believe by means of what authority requires them to believe. All they accomplish, however, is to vindicate the special privilege of the prevailing idea. That, being free while its rivals are bound, can develop confirming structures from which its rivals are restrained. Such restraint, moreover, is a disadvantage also to the favored idea. For ur'.ss the latter is continuously exercised by being subjected to free inquiry, it lapses—even if true—from a living truth into a dead dogma. That which keeps an idea alive, which saves it from atrophying into "the deep slumber of decided opinion," is doubt. Since knowledge is a consequence of discussion and controversy, doubt is an intellectual duty. Truth needs doubt for its survival and growth. The protection of the doubter, fairness, sportsmanship, equal liberty for the different—no matter how weak and foolish at first sight—are to be counted hence as preconditions of the search for truth. In them consists the "morality of public discussion."

When free to move, the truth-searching mind—which, when under arrest by authoritarian police power, tends to divert toward the sophistries, personalities, and invective which authority itself regularly employs—recovers its initial direction. The competition of beliefs for truth achieves the openness, the urbanity, the spirit of sportsmanship and fair play which we hold to be intrinsic to the method of science and the ways of art. The desires and ways of the authoritarian spirit are, however, inveterate, and where it is too weak to coerce, it will claim the guarantees of equal liberty until such a time as it feels strong enough to take power and destroy that equality. Although commonly the spirit of a religious society, it may express the operations of any: political, economic, scientific. Societies working thus will declare to the freer society which shelters and nourishes them: "We have the Truth, and we alone have the Truth. You, on your own showing, have it not. You are but searching for the truth. So long as you are the stronger, you must on your own principles tolerate and protect us. When, however, we have ourselves become the stronger, our principles require us to abolish the equal liberty to which we owe our present strength, and to proscribe you. Error has not the same rights as Truth."

V

John Mill has made sufficiently clear the potentiality of corruption and death to the very truth whose unconditional survival its champions seek thus to guarantee. Of course, it is no more true that those who take truth for something ever to be seeking have no truth, than that those who have a motor car and look for an airplane have no means of transportation. It is that they seek a vehicle which can give them faster, smoother, safer transportation. Their search is an aspect of experience taken at its face value, with its changes and chances, its diversifications and innovations accepted as realities and not appearances. The world of experience so appreciated is an open world. Freedom is inward to it. Our cognitions of it can and do take such account of it that some come to grips with it more successfully than others, and lead to alterations of it which do make it a better place to live in. Those who take account of this quality of our experience decline to be estopped by the deadly stasis of a final cognition or a final truth, even as a compensatory ideal. They regard the agonists of such finality as men afraid of freedom, whose fears both build a keep for their own minds and drive them to cruel aggressions against the freedom of other minds. They battle to contain the logic of inquiry in a grammar of assent, and to shut all divergences of the future in their own reproductions of the past. If they trusted their own truths more, they would be willing that they meet other men's truths on equal terms. Their doubt is of another kind than the doubt which John Mill commends and which is the hopeful dynamic of all the sciences. Their doubt is the deep despairing doubt of the fearful and agonized conscience. They do not, at bottom, trust the truth whose salvation they preach. Those who really and completely trust their own truths do allow error the same right as truth. The measure of their own certainty is the freedom they allow the opposition. On the record, to threaten or abolish that equal liberty is to poison the common life at the source, to mortify truth where belief maintains it and to enthrone error where doubt challenges it. It works by imposing a stasis upon the search for truth and the hope for good. Compromise with this working principle has regularly led to flagrant betrayals of mankind. This I take to be the meaning of Max Otto's words which I quote at the opening of this essay.

4

Social Philosophy: Its Method and Purpose

EDUARD C. LINDEMAN

Professor Emeritus, New York School of Social Work

IN A CONVERSATION with the late Professor Charles Horton Cooley, I announced my intention of devoting myself thenceforth to the study of philosophy—not philosophy per se, but philosophy as an instrument for making more effective use of social facts. He smiled and said: "You know, of course, what they'll say about you, don't you?" ("They" in this case meant my fellow social scientists.) When I responded in the negative, he said, "Why, they'll say you're a renegade sociologist." One may infer from this remark that some people regard social philosophers as sociologists gone wrong.

One of Mark Twain's friends, noting his dislike of hunting rabbits and cockfights and his vigorous defense of the Chinese and Polynesians, insisted that he, Mark Twain, was more of a social philosopher than a humorist.[1] A social philosopher defined in this manner becomes, then, a person who is softhearted toward animals and exploited humans.

I once overheard still another remark which carried a slightly contemptuous definition of a living social philosopher. "He is nothing," said the critic of the philosopher, "but a reformer who

---

[1] *The Times of Melville and Whitman,* by Van Wyck Brooks, p. 286.

expresses his goals in the polite and inoffensive language of philosophy." The assumption here seems to be that if this philosopher had
been "tough-minded," he might have fitted more readily the pattern
of a labor leader than that of a scholar. Or the implied meaning
may have been that social philosophers are persons who care more
about social reform than they do about technical philosophy.

According to the "kernel of truth" theory, one should examine
these derogatory statements carefully in order to determine whether
or not they bear any relation to fact. If the obvious animus of some
of these statements is removed, will the remaining charges include
elements of truth? If I may be permitted to transpose some of the
meanings involved, my answer must be affirmative. A social philosopher turns out to be a person who genuinely cares for human beings
and their welfare, who strives to include factual material taken from
the social sciences as basic components of his thought, and who is
seeking appropriate avenues for social change. I deny, however,
the implication that the social philosopher must automatically be
relegated to the genteel tradition. There is nothing inherently in-
congruous in the social philosopher who is also a social actionist.
Indeed, I should go even further and insist that it is practically impossible to play the role of social philosopher without assuming at
times the hazards of social action. It is of the essence of social
philosophy that facts, values, and actions shall somehow be blended.

Social philosophy is philosophy applied to social situations. Where
else can philosophy be applied? If philosophy is to remain the unexercised possession of the individual philosopher, what function
does it perform? It may purify his mind, sharpen his logic, clarify his
sense of the good and the beautiful—but what utility do these refinements of the insulated person serve? Is he, the philosopher, expected merely to regurgitate these wisdoms in his classroom, in
learned books or in solitary conversations with himself? Or is he
expected to put his wisdom to the test, to insert his values in equations of action? The moment he chooses this latter alternative, he
becomes a social philosopher even though the test apply only to his
family circle. In brief, philosophy in action becomes social philoso-

phy since it must then function in relation to more than one person. When the philosopher becomes one of the units in an action sequence, he will have entered the laboratory of applied philosophy.

It should be granted that social philosophers of the breed described above will of necessity be persons possessing specific qualities. They will be, for example, persons who have abandoned the mood of neutrality. In the social matrix of issues which cry for resolution, social philosophers must take sides. The luxury of indecision and of hesitant tentativeness can no longer be enjoyed. Indulgence of perpetual postponement comes to an end. Adversaries, in the Miltonian sense,[2] will be encountered; and among these will be found persons whose philosophies bear no relation to books, philosophies of experience rather than of learning, philosophies acquired in the "dust and heat" of practical living. And there will be disappointments, tragic even to the limits of utter failure, for wisdom is not the only ingredient which determines the outcome of social issues. Greed, ignorance, stupidity, and downright ill will are also involved, and among these negatives the philosopher's virtues must be made to shine. The hazards are real and formidable. I think Emerson must have had something like this in mind when he wrote in his journal: "A college professor should be elected by setting all the candidates loose on a miscellaneous gang of young men taken at large from the street. . . . Let him see if he could interest these rowdy boys in the meaning of a list of words." [3]

If the social philosopher happens to be also a teacher who anticipates—or hopes—that some of his pupils will become applied philosophers, he will be led to new ways of teaching. No longer will the leisurely journey through the history of philosophy and the amusing disputes among philosophers seem appropriate. His students will expect more of him. They will expect him to know what issues are

---

[2] As for example when Milton wrote: "I cannot praise a fugitive and cloistered virtue unexercised and unbreathed, which never sallies forth and seeks its adversary, but shrinks out of the race where that immortal garland is to be run for, not without heat and dust."

[3] Vol. VII, p. 224.

paramount in their lives and in the society of which they are a part, and they will be eager to have these very situations brought to the classroom. In the process of dealing with living issues, the philosopher's tools will be sharpened and put to new uses. They, the students, will wish to know, for example, what varieties and gradations of knowledge are embedded in propositions leading to action. This will be an epistemological question—but no longer of the classical type leading to interminable theoretical discussions in which transcendental and empirical knowing are pitted against each other. The task now is to sort out those portions of knowledge which belong to tested fact, to science, those which are sheer propaganda—that is, camouflaged falsehoods—and those which have been empirically derived but which now need to be tested in the light of new experience. This is epistemology at work, and it will be seen that the discipline no longer remains pure and categorical. Validity of knowledge now takes its place in a constellation which includes logic plus ethics. Elements which are true will be put over against others which represent that which is desirable and that which is feasible, since the entire procedure is designed to lead to reflective action. Thus the four elementary tools of philosophy—namely, epistemology, logic, ethics, and aesthetics—are put to work, not as specialized perspectives, but as partners in a team.

The disciplines of philosophy operate through the instrumentality of persons. But the disciplines cannot work in collaboration unless philosophers know how to collaborate. Another dimension of the social philosopher is thus brought to light: he must be the kind of person who enjoys joint problem-solving. This means working with other philosophers; but it also means working with scientists, administrators, politicians, technicians, and plain ordinary citizens. The social philosopher takes his place in a wide variety of groups. In each context he is expected to assist in deriving appropriate policies for the achievement of valid ends. He may at one moment be requested to give counsel with respect to the establishment of a neighborhood center in the community where he lives, and at the next to add his wisdom to the formation of world government. These are problems of the same general character, differing only in degree. Knowledge and skill required in one will be transferable to the other. But the requisite skills and knowledge cannot be learned in a study or a library, nor through continuing theoretical discussions with other philosophers. A basic consideration for applied philosophy is not disputatious competence or dialectical cunning but rather capacity for concerted reflection leading to co-operative ventures.

In the above paragraphs I may have appeared to make invidious comparisons between applied and theoretical philosophy, as if the former were of a higher order than the latter. This discrimination holds only when the question is one of practical and immediate uses of philosophy. Applied philosophers cannot, however, separate themselves completely from their theoretical brethren, those who philosophize outside the realm of action. The nourishment which comes from theoretical philosophy is necessary if only to keep applied philosophers from becoming repetitious and opportunistic. The qualities of a social philosopher which have been discussed above are germane for those philosophers motivated by a desire to put philosophy to the action test. So long as others are content to devote themselves wholly to thought divorced from use, it matters little whether they are congenial to the company of collaborators or are misanthropic individualists. I do, however, resent the contrary assumption —namely, the oft-heard claim that philosophers who deal with practical issues are not genuine philosophers. I once heard a captious critic assert that John Dewey could not possibly be considered a true philosopher since he devoted so much energy to the practical problem of how best to educate children. The inference here is, presumably, that if Dewey had confined his attention to philosophers rather than teachers of children, he would have automatically attained to the stature of true philosophy. But if philosophers speak only to philosophers, what they say will never be used. If practical and theoretical philosophers stopped calling each other names, they might rid their craft of certain stigmas, not the least being the charge that most philosophers practice an incestuous trade, occupying themselves chiefly with an exchange of footnotes. No, I do not disparage the philosopher-scholar who is unequipped by nature or inclination to engage in action, nor even those who purposely choose to devote themselves entirely to study, so long as they do not condemn others who have elected to labor elsewhere. In a proper division of labor they supplement and complement each other.

II

Thus far I have spoken as though social philosophers function only in relation to social issues which are vague and general. There are, however, certain technical areas within which social philosophers operate continuously, seeking values and suggesting policies. These specialized spheres which belong definitely to social philosophy are (a) eugenics, (b) euthenics, (c) economics, (d) government, (e) ideologies, and (f) the social uses of law. Perhaps a single question derived from each of these categories will suffice to illustrate its relation to philosophy:

(a) Should each nation control its population in such manner as to bring about a balance between standard of living and population increase? If so, what values are involved?

(b) Should the state assume responsibility for such environmental factors as health, sanitation, recreation, penology, and education? If so, what ends are to be sought?

(c) What form of economy is most suitable for a democratic society?

(d) What antidotes for bureaucracy are likely to sustain a healthy relation between the citizen and his government?

(e) What assumptions of value underlie the various competing ideologies of our time?

(f) In what manner may law be utilized as an instrument for social change?

The social philosopher's quest in each of the above inquiries is to discover a basis for public policy. Each question includes an examination of ends, a search for appropriate means, and a method for validating both ends and means. The problems themselves emerge from experience. When philosophers attempt to aid in the solution of such problems, they find it necessary to deal with two varieties of knowledge—namely, facts as revealed by the various social sciences, and values as posited by thinkers, some of whom will be philosophers. In other words, the social philosopher finds himself shuttling back and forth between science on the one hand and philosophy on the other, but he is never able to rest at either point. Indeed, he may not enjoy the privilege of confining himself to these two foci of interest: he must add another dimension, namely, a pragmatic regard for that which is feasible as well as that which is desirable. No good can come from solutions which cannot be put into practice.

Social philosophers who do not adapt themselves to the experimental mood may, of course, continue to philosophize. They may construct imaginative Utopias which neither they nor anyone else regards seriously. Such constructs are not entirely useless, however, since other philosophers of a more practical turn of mind may find in them certain suggested values which may be put to the test in actual situations.

The question of values continues to intrude itself into this discussion, and this is, perhaps, the place to indicate the type of perplexity which confronts the social philosopher whose purpose is to put knowledge to use. He will, obviously, find values in multiple sources—in religion, secular philosophy, science, literature and the arts, and in ideological affirmatives. No singular source of values will suffice for the philosopher who deals with such complex problems as suggested on page 56. But the social philosopher will inevitably find himself moving towards a theory of value which conforms with his practical aims.

When the literature on values is scrutinized, one discovers that the basic theories proposed fall into one or another, or a combination, of the following hypotheses:

(a) Values inhere in objects.
(b) Values derive from man's desires.

(c) Values stem from the mind of God.

(d) Values are contextual emergents from experience.[4]

It is difficult for me to comprehend how the social philosopher who deals with practical affairs can avoid acceptance of the last of these theories of value. If values are not in this contextual sense anticipatory derivatives of experience, the social philosopher will of necessity become a dogmatist. He can thenceforth function only in authoritarian societies. If he no longer expects values to emerge from experiments which he proposes, he will be obliged to make an artificial distinction between means and ends. His ends will be static and his means dynamic. If he possesses dictatorial power, he may be able to impose his ends upon a timid and obedient people. In this case, he will finally reach an impasse because the means utilized will convert and distort his *a priori* ends. He will either be forced to alter his immediate ends or resort to perpetual postponement of his original ends. Would it not be preferable to assume at the outset that when good ends are sought and consonant means are employed for their realization, new values are likely to emerge?

A social philosopher inevitably becomes a critic of the culture of which he is a part. If his criticism tends towards negativism, he will sooner or later find himself separated from the ethos of his own society. When this happens he becomes an *emigré* and hence loses that sense of loyalty to his own culture which makes of criticism a creative act. Caught in this situation, the social philosopher will soon discover that he has been insulated from the functional aspects of his society and will thereafter operate in an expanding vacuum. He will cease to be a collaborator; detached from the "dust and heat" where issues arise and values are posited, he will lose certain insights, certain connections with the processes of his society; a significant form of reality will thus escape him.

---

[4] This schematic arrangement of schools of thought concerned with value is a simplification of Henry N. Wieman's discussion in his *The Source of Human Good*. His scheme, however, includes seven and possibly eight separate explanations of value-beliefs.

The reality which lies embedded in those important issues which give life and vitality to a culture is the social philosopher's object of inquiry. In an earlier section I spoke of the demands which students make of their teachers in social-philosophy courses, and it will be recalled that I then stated that students expect philosophy to deal with *real* issues. Perhaps I can now make clearer what some of the methods and purposes of social philosophy are if certain issues in American life are brought to the fore.

To speak of all issues as though they were equal in weight and importance is to avoid a preliminary skill—namely, the skill of discrimination between those issues which are primary and persistent and those which are derivative and become difficult only because the primary issues remain unresolved. In the United States, primary issues tend to become Constitutional questions and hence appear with cyclical regularity before the Supreme Court. These are, for the most part, issues which involve a definition of the *powers* of the state. Secondary issues arise from immediate needs, are largely legislative in character, and involve definitions of *functions* of the state. Utilizing this preliminary discrimination, it may be said that the character of the American economy is a primary issue whereas the problem of building houses for our people is secondary. The social philosopher's task is to reach a reasonable conviction respecting both primary and secondary issues and to reveal the interrelations between the two. The amount and quality of work to be done in these areas by philosophers may become clearer if a partial list of the two types of issues is inserted here:

(A) Issues which are primary, qualitative, and indicative of the relative powers of the state:
   (1) The authority of business, industry, and finance *versus* the authority of government in determining economic policies.
   (2) The capacity of the federal government to enforce the terms of the Bill of Rights *versus* the recalcitrance of individual commonwealths and certain private associations.
   (3) The tendency to discriminate against certain citizens on

account of their religion, race, color, sex, or national origin *versus* Constitutional guarantees of equality.

(4) The authority of government to conserve our natural resources *versus* the exploitation of those resources for private profit.

(5) The struggle between private enterprise on the one hand and the right of governmental control on the other. (This issue might also be described as the attempt to define the nature of the American economy.)

(6) The state *versus* the church.

(7) Isolationism *versus* positive international collaboration.

To the extent that trends may be discovered in relation to the above issues, it becomes possible to denote the character of American culture. These are issues of the type which tend to persist, to become chronic, and to arise in new guises under varying circumstances. These issues are descriptive of basic values.

(B) Secondary or derivative issues which arise because of immediate needs and become difficult of solution largely because of the unresolved status of such primary issues as are listed above:

(1) The need to build houses for families *versus* the inability of families to pay for houses or to pay the rents needed to make private home-building a profitable enterprise.

(2) The need for extending adequate medical care to those citizens who cannot under present circumstances buy such care *versus* the demands of the medical profession to perpetuate its present fee system.

(3) The need to extend basic social securities to expanding numbers of citizens *versus* adherence to the doctrine of self-reliance.

(4) The need to lower the national crime and delinquency record *versus* the tradition of lawlessness, inability of enforcing agencies to co-operate, and ineptness in teaching morality.

(5) The need to equalize educational opportunities throughout the nation *versus* the fear of educational regimentation.

(6) The need to control inflation through price controls *versus* the fear of economic regimentation and a comprehensive system of black markets.

(7) The need for a free flow of goods in international trade *versus* the traditional conceptions of protective tariffs.

It will be noted that with respect to these issues it is not difficult to secure agreement regarding the ends in view. The ordinary citizen is in favor of houses, health, security, obedience to law, educational opportunities for all, lower prices, and free trade, but he is troubled about the right and wrong ways of attaining these goals. He is motivated in his attitudes largely by fears, and in most instances these fears are associated with the unresolved status of the primary issues. He is uncertain about the direction in which he wishes to move. He is restrained from engaging in experimentation because he is not sure where trial and error will carry his country.

It is easily seen that both sets of issues furnish the raw material out of which American political life is constructed. Politicians deal with these issues in the light of partisan advantage. Propagandists utilize these issues for purposes of confusion. How, then, does the philosopher set to work when confronted with problems of this nature? At what points does he exercise his professional right to participate? Which elements of these problems belong especially to the realm of his competence?

The philosopher's approach to the basic issues of his society may be either that of an *a priori* conviction regarding the ends to be sought, or a similarly abrupt rejection of the methods proposed. In either instance he thus enters the equation with a pronouncement, and departs. All too frequently, it seems to me, this describes the behavior of philosophers in relation to public issues. They are consulted as though they were oracles; they make their pronouncements, and then retreat to their shelters. Although this is not the appropriate place to enter upon detailed descriptions of other types of philosophical approaches to social problems, it does seem proper to point out one or two alternatives.

In the first place, it seems to me reasonable to expect a philosopher to make a contextual analysis of an issue before he expresses a judgment with respect to either ends or means. His first question is: "What kind of situation is this and what are its principal factors?" If, then, he expects his notions to be taken seriously, he must make inquiries respecting the feasibility of the various solutions suggested; he will then proceed to deal with the problem from the viewpoint of human needs, and next, perhaps, from the viewpoint of values. By this time he will be in a position to construct a number of graded scales indicating the range of possible alternatives. If, during this process, our philosopher has been sufficiently pragmatic to suit the demands of the practical persons who will be obliged to assume responsibility for whatever action is indicated, he will be able to induce his colleagues to undertake a careful scrutiny of the probable consequences which might flow from various solutions. His chief aim having been to keep the situation fluid until a proper sifting of evidence and an examination of relationships have been made, he, the philosopher, is now in position to prevent further errors which result when people assume that all experimentalism ends once a decision has been taken. Those who conduct an experiment should also be prepared to appraise its consequences and, if necessary, to reformulate the proposition for purposes of further experimentation.

The above represents an elementary approach to social issues and might appear to most technical philosophers as being too naïve, too simple. I have purposely omitted many of the resources which a philosopher might invoke if he were involved in a joint problem-solving venture, since my main purpose was to demonstrate how natural and congenial this type of functioning would be if philosophers thought of themselves as participants rather than as observers in the social drama of their time and place. It is easy enough for a philosopher to love truth in the abstract, but he will never know whether or not his devotion to truth is sincere until he has attempted to put it to work in living situations.[5]

III

Social situations, when analyzed, invariably turn out to be equations of interaction between a person and another person, a person and a group, or a group and another group. In recent times these varieties of interaction have all been subsumed under the title "human relations." Tensions, frictions, and conflicts in the areas of human relations tend to increase in spite of the fact that all human beings tend to become related to each other in more ways and are hence more dependent upon each other. It is this paradox which has brought the question of human relations to the fore and has made of it one of the chief concerns of social scientists of this age. Is this an area in which philosophers might also be expected to participate and to make contributions? So acute has the question of human relations become in American life that demands are made by citizens that children should be subjected to human-relations courses in the public schools. Hence, the question has already become a public issue. Have philosophers anything to say about it?

The principal factor involved in human relations is understanding. Negroes and whites must understand each other. Employers and trade unionists must understand each other. Americans and Russians must understand each other. These appeals one hears on every side—but what, precisely, does understanding mean? And where does the philosopher's insight impinge upon the process of understanding?

These are important but subtle questions and, if I am not mistaken, they will occupy the attention of thoughtful people over a very long period of time. The plain truth of the matter seems to be

---

[5] Elsewhere I have described in greater detail the operations of philosophy in connection with an actual social situation. See "Science and Philosophy: Sources of Humanitarian Faith" in *Social Work as Human Relations* (New York: Columbia University Press, 1949), commemorating the fiftieth anniversary of the New York School of Social Work.

that understanding becomes more difficult in direct ratio to the increase of interdependence, and that the larger the number of relations becomes, the greater will be the difficulty of understanding. Stated otherwise, every increment of complexity will bring a corresponding decrease in understanding. Since this is the issue upon which peace ultimately depends, one must assume that philosophers will regard it as a subject relevant to their interests.

The first approach to this intricate question of understanding is, obviously, to discover how many varieties of understanding are involved in modern living.[6] If A does what B tells him to do, A has understood B. But what happens when A refuses to do what B commands? If A happens to be a traveler and B is a railroad time-table, A will have understood B if he boards the right train. But, the reader will have noticed that information desks at railroad and airplane and bus stations tend to increase, and that their anxious patrons appear to be beset with more uncertainties. If A is traveling during a special season of the year, he will need to know how to distinguish between daylight saving time and standard time. Curiously enough, this task seems to be difficult even for relatively sophisticated persons. There are other complications: schedules are altered more frequently than in former times; certain trains will admit passengers only if they have made seat reservations in advance; there are now more gradations of accommodation; and so on.

But the above type of understanding is simple indeed when compared with the situation when A happens to belong to one distinct cultural background while B comes from one with marked differences. In this instance, both A and B arrive upon the scene loaded with accumulations of customs, mores, taboos, and standards which seem to each reasonable and appropriate. In fact, A and B are likely to believe that their respective cultures are superior, founded upon more valid principles. Surely, philosophy and its disciplines may be used in situations of this type. The use of the word "valid" in the

---

[6] Indeed, an excellent beginning has already been made and will be found under the title "Why Discussions Go Astray," by Irving J. Lee, in *Etc.*, Vol. IV, No. 2 (1946).

above sentence indicates that values are involved, and where values are important there the philosopher is, or should be, present. Is it possible to have peace in a world of plural values? If so, upon what terms? Is it not noticeable that wherever one encounters rigidity and dogmatism with respect to values, there human relations tend to deteriorate? Relations, that is, tend to deteriorate as between those who hold dogmas and those who do not, or between those who adhere to different dogmas. Those within the dogmatic circle seem actually to improve their human relations since it now appears that conflict diminishes. Indeed it sometimes diminishes to the vanishing point, because authorities will no longer tolerate deviations. What are the probable consequences to personality development where authoritative dogmas are imposed upon all? And what is to be done about dogma-driven groups which exist in societies dedicated to freedom? How many "islands" of absolutism may be tolerated in a democratic society? Or, if tolerated, what rules of conduct need to be invoked? These are in essence philosophic questions, but neither the purposes nor the methods of philosophy have thus far been brought to bear with effectiveness upon these and related issues.

IV

Since I have elsewhere dealt with questions involving the philosophy of democracy,[7] I shall mention here only one phase of this enterprise. During the past decade I have devoted a considerable portion of my time and energy to the task of constructing a set of partially empirical values which seem to me to be necessary if democracy is to become thoroughly incorporated in the learning process.[8] Our inherited, non-empirical, eighteenth-century, democratic ideals—liberty, equality, and fraternity—do not lend themselves readily to the teaching situation. We may repeat them, and we may point out the different ways in which these values appear

---

[7] For example, in "Sources of Value for Modern Man," *Baldwin-Wallace College Bulletin*.

[8] Happily, it was Max Otto, the man to whom this volume is dedicated, who gave me the opportunity to explore this problem with a selected group of students at the University of Wisconsin during the year 1946.

at different periods of history. There are times when confronted with the repetitious incantation of these ideals that I am reminded of Anatole France's character who exclaimed: "Monsieur, when we have called beauty beautiful, truth true, and justice just, we shall have said nothing at all." I am not intimating that these values have no further utility in promoting democracy. These are important ideals, especially to those who have experienced them, but they need to be buttressed by other rules of conduct which may be in part validated by science, and in part by reference to ongoing experiences of daily living.

Why, for example, do exponents of democracy insist upon diversity as a value superior to uniformity? Why is it that proponents of democracy lay so much stress upon the necessity of keeping ends and means in approximate consonance? Why do advocates of democracy rule out perfectionism and the either-or principle? If diversity, the means-ends principle, and the doctrine of the partial operation of ideals are inherent in democratic living, how are these disciplines of democracy to be taught? These are questions which, so it seems to me, the philosopher of these fateful times cannot avoid unless he is prepared to be classified as a "fugitive" from the basic "race" of his age, the "race" whose outcome will determine his future privilege to live as a free man—that is, to be a philosopher.

5

Postulational Methods in the Social Sciences

ARNOLD DRESDEN

Professor of Mathematics, Swarthmore College

THE RUIN WHICH THE ATOMIC BOMB rained on Hiroshima has been
recorded for posterity in the epic of John Hersey. No one has an
excuse for being unaware of the terrific impact which this tremendous advance in the utilization of nuclear energies is having on
the physical aspects of life on this earth. It is the result of carrying
over into human activities some of the important scientific discoveries of the past decades, placed in a setting which gave it high
dramatic power. There is no question as to the effect it produced.
Nevertheless, steadily renewed emphasis on the convulsive aspects
of these developments is essential. For, in spite of the deep disturb-
ances they have caused, in spite of John Hersey's powerful account,
in spite of the Bikini tests, there does not seem to emerge a determination on the part of mankind to adjust the conditions of life
on this planet to the profound changes which the advent of nuclear
power among man's resources has brought about.

It is a depressing realization that our standards of behavior have
been so little affected. Many years ago, Samuel McChord Crothers
illustrated in a striking manner the effect of changes in the material environment upon man's standards of virtue. If you are at the
seashore in the midst of a storm, he said, and see a ship in distress

some distance out, if then you wring your hands in despair and clamor for aid, without doing anything further for those in danger, no blame attaches to your virtue. But, when someone comes running up to you and says, "Here is a boat; let us get into it and try to rescue those people over there," then your mere clamor and wringing of hands is no longer a virtuous response to the situation. Then a different response is called for.

Is there nothing within our power except to cry out in distress at the dangers to which nuclear energy exposes us? Are there no measures which will effectively take account of the fundamental shifts in human existence which these recent developments have occasioned?

It must of course be admitted that we have not been without revolt or advice. The development of the atomic bomb was not an isolated phenomenon; rather has it been a climax—thus far the greatest climax—of a long series of inventions, applications of fundamental science to various techniques, some merely destructive, others possessing possibilities of contributing to human welfare, but all of them deeply disturbing to the kind of life to which we have been accustomed. People have felt their "normal existence" threatened, and they have rebelled against accepting the new inventions as inescapable and commanding features of the life of the future. These new things have been called inventions of the devil, materialistic excesses, outgrowths of the neglect of traditional religion; they have been looked upon as aspects of life to be shunned, if not ignored, rather than as phenomena to be accepted and turned to man's advancement. Thus we have heard it advocated that a "scientific holiday" be declared. We have been told that mankind pleads for a chance to catch up with all the disturbing inventions and gadgets. It has been repeated over and over again, from the chancel and the pulpit, from the rostrum and the soapbox, in print and over the air, that our troubles arise from the lack of social responsibility of the scientists, from their failure to feel concern for the uses which are made of their discoveries and inventions, from their indifference to humanity. Occasionally blame has been heaped upon the social scientists, the social engineers, for their failure to catch up with modern life, to adjust the social machinery to the changed environment, to adopt in their own fields of study the methods which have led to such brilliant success in the fields of the physical sciences and of engineering.

Apart from the fact that, in some groups at least, the demand for a scientific holiday has its roots in an instinctive fear that all the new inventions will disturb the social equilibrium which is so satisfactory to the privileged ones on top of the pile,[1] it is another manifestation of the "prohibition" attitude which, in spite of the disastrous experience of the twenties, still has a tremendous hold on people. The "spirit of denial" is still strong: there are always those who want to keep the birds from singing, the children from playacting, the artists from living in a world of their imagination. The conflict between those who ask the scientists, the engineers, and the inventors to slow up, and those who urge the social engineers to hasten forward, is of particular interest for the present discussion.

I cannot free myself from a picture which persists in coming before me when I think of this conflict. It shows two children walking along a road, one pulling and the other laboriously pushing a well-loaded baby carriage. The one in front runs and jumps along as fast as he can. The other is desperately trying to hang on, shouting and wailing, "Wait for me, Willy!" But Willy goes along merrily, sometimes leaving the other to push the entire load, throwing back a smile and a yell, "Come along, you slowpoke Benny." Between them the baby carriage jolts and shakes, to the severe discomfort of its contents. Perhaps someone will come along to suggest to Benny that he might learn from Willy how to increase his speed, and to Willy the need of getting control of his exuberance, before the baby is spilled out of the carriage along with the eggs, the milk, and the chops which the boys were supposed to bring home.

In this state of affairs it may indeed be useful to call attention to some aspects of the physical and the natural sciences which may

---

[1] There is in this demand a suggestive analogy with the opposition with which new technical devices have to contend.

be of value to the social scientist. It is the conviction of many that significant advancement in the field of the social sciences can be expected to result from their use of the scientific method.[2] This point of view has been advocated by many writers for some time. The variety of meanings attached to "scientific method" opens the way for a great diversity of opinion. It is not the intention to consider it in the present discussion.

It is our purpose to direct attention to the fundamental procedures of mathematics. The basic character of this discipline for the whole field of science has long been recognized, at least in theory. The fact that it has its roots in the substratum of human experience points to the possibility that the social sciences may also derive something of value from a closer acquaintance with its basic methods. Although mathematics is plentifully abused for its abstractness, its remoteness from "real life," the subject enjoys on the other hand a certain respect; it is frequently given credit for being trustworthy and dependable in a high degree. "Mathematical certainty" has a quality of its own in the minds of many people. "It is mathematically certain that higher wages in the coal industry will lead to a general rise in the cost of living"; it is "mathematically certain that a child allowed to visit the movies without restriction will grow up with criminal tendencies"; and so on. Who has not heard such statements? And who has the courage to persist in an argument when he has been confronted with such Jovian arguments?

Whence does mathematics derive this quality of finality, so much desired by workers in the social sciences? It is my judgment that the greatest strength of mathematics lies in its abstract character, which invests the subject with a quality of universality. In its systematic development the logical element is strongly emphasized and kept distinct from the factual interpretation and content. This

---

[2] See, e.g., Condon, in *Science*, for June 25, 1948, pp. 659–665: "In short, the greatest contribution to real security that science can make is through the extension of the scientific method to the social sciences and a solution of the problem of complete avoidance of war."

thesis we hope to elucidate and to develop in the following pages. Perhaps we are not far wrong in saying that, when people refer to a conclusion as "mathematically certain," their essential meaning is that the conclusion is capable of logical demonstration. Indeed, it is unquestionably one of the characteristics of a mathematical discipline that it presents demonstrations of its assertions. Its proofs, followed by the magic symbol Q.E.D., give the subject a quality of validity more impressive to the layman than the procedures current in other fields of knowledge.

It is an aspiration of workers in the various natural sciences and it is gradually becoming an ambition of social scientists to attain comparable validity for their conclusions. It will therefore suit our purpose to analyze the way in which mathematics "demonstrates," to trace out the road along which the natural sciences travel to provide their general conclusions with a mathematical basis, to make clear the nexus which makes possible the linking of their empirical procedures with the theoretical structures which they set up on paper and into which their experimental conclusions have to fit. Such an analysis has little novelty for the mathematician, or for the natural scientist. It may have significance for the social scientist, in so far as it may indicate a possible procedure for his field; it may interest the philosopher as a means of closing the gap between Willy and Benny before the carriage is wrecked.

Perhaps a personal word is not out of place in this commemorative volume. It has been one of the abiding interests of Max Otto to study the contributions of workers in the physical as well as in the natural sciences to the understanding of human problems, to subject their conclusions to critical, logical analysis, to point out hopeful possibilities for carrying over into our everyday life the ideals which have inspired the great scientists of all times. Many have been the occasions on which an utterance of a "leading man of science" was discussed, tested by the standards of the most illustrious names in the field, shorn of adventitious importance or false dignity. It used to be my part to apply mathematical criteria of reasoning, to point out the bearing which mathematical procedures had on the problem under discussion. Max Otto would then compare the criticism and remarks I could offer with his own philosophical judgments, to determine whether they would bear them out or whether they would weaken his philosophical position. Thus, the theme which has been chosen for my part in this volume dedicated to Max Otto carries forward the discussions which he and I used to have more than twenty years ago; it bears witness to the influence which his thinking has had upon his friends.

The distinctive contribution which mathematics makes to scientific methodology, quite apart from the tools which it fashions for scientific investigation, consists in the explicit formulation of postulational bases for its theories. It is well know that this postulational procedure goes back at least to Euclid; it is perhaps less well recognized that its elaboration and formal development did not take place until the latter part of the nineteenth century. It was not until then that the full effects of the introduction of the non-Euclidean geometries, of the general theory of sets, and of the arithmetization of analysis made themselves felt. The appearance of David Hilbert's *Grundlagen der Geometrie* (1899) is for this reason one of the important milestones in the development of mathematics.

Hilbert's presentation of the foundations of geometry begins with "things" called points, lines, and planes. Concerning these "things," a number of postulates are stated—that is to say, sharply and unequivocally stated conditions which these "things" have to satisfy. No meaning is to be attached to the "things," no demonstration of the postulates is therefore called for. This procedure illustrates the thought behind Bertrand Russell's aphorism that mathematics is the discipline in which we "do not know what we are talking about, nor whether what we say is true." It is followed, with slight modifications, in all treatments of the Foundations of Geometry (Pasch, Pieri, Veblen, and others), as well as in the numerous postulational studies for various domains of arithmetic, algebra, and analysis (Dickson, Huntington, Sheffer, and many others). Perhaps the method reached a climax in the *Formulario di Mate-*

matica of Peano and in the *Principia Mathematica* of Whitehead and Russell.

We proceed now to a somewhat closer examination of this procedure in the hope of finding a clue pointing towards the possibility of its application in the social sciences. We must begin by observing that the points, lines, planes of the geometries, the elements of the sets in algebra and analysis, are not really the disembodied entities which their creators placed on the scene. The fact that even the most abstract studies of this sort are always systems of postulates *for* this, that, or the other fields; the fact that we have Foundations *of Geometry*, "complete sets of postulates *for* the theories of positive integral and of positive rational numbers"; [3] the fact that the first ninety-odd pages of *Principia Mathematica* serve to orient the reader into the meaning of the abstract treatment which is to follow—all these point unmistakably to the conclusion that the "things" to which no meaning is to be attached are not the pale ghosts, the words without content, which the architects of these structures want to use as their building blocks. It is easy to say that the "points" and "lines," the "between relation" of geometry, the "positive integers" and the "addition" of algebra—which are the undefined concepts in terms of which the postulates are formulated—are not to be invested with meaning and should in particular be kept free from contamination with the meanings which are traditionally associated with these words. But where is the human being who can thus dissociate himself from all previous commerce with these words and from the contexts in which they have become embedded? Are we able to step at will out of the experiences which we have had, can we free ourselves from the intellectual environment in which we have become encrusted? Could we manage such a bootstrap feat? But, even if we did accomplish this acrobatic trick, what would we then do with these freed notions, unattached to anything in our experience? What would determine the choice of postulates to which they have to be subjected?

---

[3] Huntington, *Transactions of the American Mathematical Society*, Vol. III (1902).

The point of view of the early axiomatists, the insistence that the primitive concepts of their theories should be free from meaning, was a natural consequence of their desire to separate the logical structure of mathematics from its traditional contents. It is only to the extent that we succeed in thus isolating the logical moments in the theories that we can hope to gain insight into their abstract structure. And, provided this method can be reduced to a realistic formulation, it is perhaps the most important contribution which mathematics can hope to make to the methodology of the social sciences.

Not to "reason from the figure" in geometry, not to accept the conclusion that an infinite series is convergent merely because it has a "physical meaning," not to accept an algebraic formula as valid merely because it has been verified in a "large number" of cases—all these are sound warnings. They constitute important methodological principles. Passing to analogical situations in the fields of social science, it might be judged unwise to accept a political or an economic theory merely because it has been successful towards a desired end in a number of instances. It might be greater wisdom not to accept the city-manager plan as *the* solution of our problem of municipal government merely because Cincinnati fared well under Dykstra, not to accept the capitalist form of production as universally desirable merely because British industry grew to a position of unprecedented power after the Industrial Revolution.

Thus it is natural that the attempt should have been made to construct abstract postulational systems in terms of symbols and of words devoid of "meaning." But it should be clear that the divorce from previous experience which the attempt implies is incapable of realization. It is certainly impossible for one who wants to construct a postulational system for a given field; and it is extremely doubtful whether anyone can acquire more than a purely formal knowledge of such a system without putting some clothes on the bare, abstract concepts. The purpose which has been set for the present discussion would certainly be a hopeless one if the effective use of the axiomatic method were contingent upon a complete devitalization of the primitive concepts. For, whatever may be possible in mathematics or in the physical sciences, we could certainly not free ourselves of the ambient atmosphere in which our social concepts have their existence. Would any social philosopher trust himself to talk about "family," "sex," "nation," "individual," without inevitably investing these words with extensive accumulations of meaning?

The potential value of the axiomatic method for the development of the social sciences does not depend, however—any more than it does for mathematics itself—upon such a make-believe separation of the scientist into an axiomatic ignorantist and a factually learned person. In order to make this statement acceptable, we shall have to examine once more the role of the axiomatic method in mathematics. The *Elements* of Euclid, the prototype of systematic logical systems, begins with *definitions* of "point," "line," and "plane." Hilbert's *Grundlagen der Geometrie* begins with the same words, but so far from their being defined, it has to be understood that they are divested of meaningful content, except in so far as the postulates which are to follow may give them meaning.

Where does the difference lie between these superficially similar presentations? While in Euclid the point, line, and plane are placed at the very beginning of the theory, we soon become aware of the fact that there is a vast substructure of experience which underlies these concepts. Thus, although he begins with point, line, etc., these concepts stand logically *in medias res;* there is no intention to separate them from the substructure. Now, the point of the present argument is precisely this, that these basic concepts are bound to occupy this central position in any system which takes into account that mathematics is after all a human enterprise, to be carried on by human beings who cannot effectively free themselves from the intellectual ballast which they have acquired, partly by racial inheritance and partly by the experiences which were theirs before they became axiomatists. It remains to indicate how the *medias res* position manifests itself in the postulation systems, in particular in Hilbert's *Grundlagen.*

This is done by saying that it shows itself in the choice of the postulates; they are expected to be postulates for geometry! If the point, line, and plane were really free from all connections with a substructure, there would be nothing to determine the choice of the postulates. The "undefined elements" would indeed be disembodied entities, not suitable material for the building of a theory.

While thus, unquestionably, a meaning of the terms must be present before postulates can be formulated, this meaning is kept *logically separate* from the content of the structure that is developed from the postulates. In the proofs, it is not the meaning of the primitive concepts to which appeal is made; it is the postulates and the consequences derived from them which have authoritative status. When the meaning of the terms does occasionally peep around the corner (and who can avoid such indiscretions when an argument is to be designed?) they do not gain any significant logical status as a result of such behavior.

It should become clear from what has just been said that the significance of the axiomatic procedure manifests itself in the insight it provides in the logical structure of a field of knowledge. Rarely, if ever, does a postulational treatment contribute to the "forward development" of a subject; a misleading form of this statement—the assertion that the postulational method does not produce any new knowledge—has been used to disparage the procedure altogether. It has to be understood that fields of knowledge for which postulational systems have been set up have not historically been developed from the postulates; they had previously acquired existence in some way, perhaps as a result of experience with actual problems. The historical development of mathematical disciplines after 1900 can be thought of as a two-way movement: from the experience to the foundations by logical analysis, and from the foundations by logical synthesis to experience in abstract formulation, and beyond.

Starting with as extensive a knowledge of an existing field as one can acquire, one looks for as simple a basis as possible from which the existing field can be developed logically without the further intervention of such previously acquired knowledge. Such a basis will of necessity consist of a set of primitive concepts (undefined terms) together with a set of postulates (unproved propositions). Every term that is introduced later must be introduced by being defined logically in terms of the primitive concepts; and every proposition which appears in the further development of the theory must be deduced logically from the postulates. One does not have to behave "as if" one did not have any previous knowledge of the "things"; but one must separate the logical development completely from this factual knowledge. In this manner, logical fallacies will be more readily detected than if the field of knowledge remains in the state of an undifferentiated accumulation of facts and principles, in which conclusions are accepted, partly on the basis of a logical argument, partly on the strength of the knowledge acquired from experience. In such an unorganized mass, in which the roles of experience and of logical deduction remain hopelessly intertwined, logically invalid doctrines may be maintained, because they have sometimes led to acceptable results. It does not appear unreasonable to think that, for this reason, a differentiation of logical procedure from experience could be of particular value in the social sciences.

Because the emphasis has always been placed on the logical structure of postulational systems, much attention has been given to their internal properties. In their construction, the consistency and the independence of the postulates have been a principal concern. Since the independence of a set of N postulates is understood to mean the consistency of the N new systems obtained by replacing any one of the given postulates by its negative,[4] these two properties of a system both involve a criterion of consistency—that is, a test for non-contradictoriness. The logical importance of such a criterion is obviously very great; of the same order of magnitude is its difficulty. It has proved to be one of the most taxing prob-

---

[4] A good many difficulties may arise in the statement of the negative of a postulate; to avoid them it is desirable to insist upon the exclusive use of "unit-postulates," whose negatives are unambiguous. E. H. Moore has introduced the concept of "complete independence"; this means the consistency of all the systems which can be obtained by replacing *one or more* of the postulates by their negatives.

lems which confronts theoretical logicians. It has received a great deal of attention in recent years; progress has been made, but much remains to be done. The independence of a system of postulates has a certain aesthetic value; not to include redundancies in the postulates is, however, also desirable apart from aesthetic considerations, especially when an application of the system is to be made.

A third requirement which postulate systems were expected to meet, particularly during the earlier period, was that of categoricalness. It is of more direct importance for our purpose than the logical problem of consistency. It is essentially a requirement of uniqueness and is therefore central when we wish to set up a postulational basis for a particular field of knowledge. The question which is involved can be formulated as follows: How can we be sure that a system of postulates can serve as a logical basis for a specified field of knowledge?

To answer this question, it is desirable to make clear what is to be understood by "interpretations" and "applications" of such a system. An "interpretation" is made when each of the primitive concepts is identified with a concept of an existing field of knowledge—that is, with a concept of which, in some sense, we have previously acquired knowledge. If, with such an identification of the primitive concepts, the postulates which have been laid down concerning them can be verified in this field of knowledge, then we call this field an "application" or an "instance" of the postulate system: the system is "applicable" to this field. The test for consistency of a set of postulates has been the existence of a field which is an "instance" of this set.

It follows from this use of the terms that every logical deduction of our postulates is logically valid in the existing field of knowledge. It does *not* follow, however, that this existing field is adequately portrayed in the abstract system; it is not sure that *all* the conclusions of which the existing field is capable can be obtained by interpretation of the deductions in the abstract system. In other words, it cannot be maintained that the system furnishes a postulational basis *for* every one of its instances. To say that a system of postulates is categorical means exactly that it is a basis *for every one* of its instances, in the following sense: If we have two different instances, A and B, of a given abstract system, these two must be isomorphic; and this in turn means that it must be possible to set up a 1–1 correspondence between the elements and relations of A and those of B, in such a way that when a relation of A holds between certain elements of A, then the corresponding relation of B will hold between the corresponding elements of B.[5]

A categorical system of postulates for a particular field of knowledge can therefore be considered as a logical abstraction of this field. Its further developments can all be interpreted so as to give conclusions valid in that field; and, conversely, every deduction of which the field is logically capable can be obtained as an interpretation of the abstract system. (In such a system, the postulates can be thought of as implicitly defining the primitive concepts.)

If a logical analysis of the kind we have discussed is to be attained for a social-science field by the methods which have proved themselves useful in mathematics, the construction of a consistent and categorical set of postulates, applicable to specified fields of social inquiry, is therefore the first necessary step.

Two remarks have to be made in closing. For the comparison of two or more different fields which have some characteristics in common, a non-categorical set of postulates may have great value. This set should be categorical for the theoretically conceivable— although perhaps not actually existing—domain common to those fields. This primary set of postulates makes possible a logical analysis of the common features of these different fields. By the introduction of one or several supplementary postulates, one could then obtain categorical sets for each of the fields in particular, thus

---

[5] A very simple example of isomorphism is the following: Let A consist of the natural numbers $1, 2, \ldots, n, \ldots$ and the relation between 3 numbers which exist when one of them is obtained by adding the other two. Let B consist of the integers $3^1, 3^2, \ldots, 3^n, \ldots$ and the relation which holds between 3 of them when one of them is obtained by multiplying the other two. Then A and B are isomorphic. For, if with any number a of A we associate the number 3^a of B, then, if $p + q = r$, we can conclude that $3^p \cdot 3^q = 3^r$.

clarifying the logical structure of the ways in which the fields are different.

The development of a postulational procedure in the social sciences obviously requires a wide acquaintaince with actually existing fields belonging to these sciences. A fertile source of such fields is provided by the studies of societies different from our own which have been made by the anthropologists in recent years. These studies can also be very useful in connection with the consistency problem and as a means of providing "interpretations" of postulate systems in the social sciences.

6

Social Planning

HORACE S. FRIES

Late Professor of Philosophy, University of Wisconsin

WE ARE BEGINNING TO REALIZE that the Industrial Revolution was also a revolution in culture and human nature. We are becoming aware of the import of the fact that the medieval folkways have been liquidated and that some substitute must be devised for them in modern society.

There are those who believe this substitute can be provided by merely refurbishing the medieval world view and adapting it to our scientific-technological culture. They see the need for the stabilization which was provided by the medieval folkways, but they deny or ignore the fact that a revolution has taken place. Medieval metaphysics and theology were doubtless integrated factors within the folkways of the period. But the neo-medievalists mistake these ideas for the eternal structure of "Reality," demanding that citizens of the modern world adjust themselves first to this transcendent order of "Being," and by this means to modern revolutionary social changes which are reduced to the order of "Appearance."

There are other advocates of social planning who recognize the reality of social change. But members of this group too frequently are inhibited or blocked at some point in their thinking by various traditional dualisms which were sharpened by the advent of science but which can be justified only in terms of pre-scientific metaphysical conceptions which are no longer tenable. Although they acknowledge the fact of social revolution, they have not fully realized its effect as an essential change in human nature itself. They realize that there is no alternative to social chaos save the *deliberate* performance of the functions which were once automatically regulated by stable and relatively fixed social customs. But they have yet to realize the full moral and aesthetic sweep of the functions demanded.

The deliberate institution of a substitute for the folkways is the function of social planning. Although the accumulation of fighting connotations around the term "planning" is a relatively recent development, it is anything but surprising that there should be great disagreement about its meaning and implications. Even those who oppose "planning" as such admit that they are not opposed to "planning correctly conceived." The explanation of this paradox is not difficult to find. The "planning" we are all for or against is seen to entail some kind of either direct or indirect control of the market, and usually this is envisaged as centralized governmental control or "interference."

It is evidently unwise to assume that there will not be more government interference and more centralized planning within the next several years. Such an assumption is almost bound to make for accelerated drift into unsuccessful planning, and therefore into increasing use of coercive power in futile efforts to secure social objectives. It is equally unwise, however, to assume that deliberate steps toward planning will automatically be successful. Yet too many planners (and proportionately more laymen who agree that planning will be expanded) are acting on this assumption.

Some ambiguities enter our concepts of planning through arbitrary limitations of the term to political or economic fields. But aside from the question of the valid distinction among fields of inquiry, the range of the concept is vague, and limited by dualistic medieval hangovers.

Dictionaries for the most part define planning as having to do with means, and leave the question of ends as extraneous. This

dictionary trait suggests the hypothesis that contemporary planners who exclude the problem of the formulation of aims from the
ongoing planning process are being inhibited by unacknowledged
and unrecognized habitual assumptions which elevate the realm of
ends exclusively to a transcendental order and leave the realm of
change as one merely of means and techniques.

These prevailing ambiguities and the contending forces growing
out of them call for an analysis of the planning context, a clarification of its assumptions and purposes, and a consideration of the
general principles by which planning is to be guided. We shall propose four general principles as necessary and—with their implied
principles—sufficient for guiding social planning.

II

In its most general sense, the aim of social planning is to provide
for the fulfillment of desires. This is so broad a statement that it
may seem innocuous. Yet it immediately sheds light on the nature
of planning, for a very evident fact about desires indicates the im-
possibility of separating means from ends: This is the fact that human desires can and do come into conflict with one another. "Child-
ishness" might be defined (oversimply) as the inability to eliminate
impossible desires from the individual's pattern of conduct or, better,
the failure to redirect them toward relevant possibilities. And mature life is a perpetual series of decisions to pursue course A in preference to course B, both of which are yet wanted. The social-physical
environment cuts off desires in notoriously crude and costly ways.
The planning enterprise cannot escape the moral responsibility of
deciding among competing wants. At the same time we should
welcome the opportunity to employ conflicts as occasions for instituting progressively richer patterns of desire.

It is an evident if unintentional ruse to reduce human desires to
groups of needs, and then simply try to plan the economic enterprise in such a way as to provide as abundantly as possible for
these needs. Hence it is refreshing to find such a statement as the
following by a distinguished planner:

A clear distinction ought to be made between what people want and what they need. It is legitimate criticism of such studies as have been made by Stuart Chase that they take as a starting point, not what people *want,* but what an impartial commentator thinks they *ought* to want. . . . The only practicable method of handling an investigation of the industrial system today is to assume that people are entitled to want what they actually do want; and to define economic efficiency as giving people what they want. Anything else involves deciding (and ultimately trying to tell people) what they ought to want, which becomes tyranny pure and simple.[1]

But our refreshment is short-lived. For the passage merely substitutes one form of escape for another. While to reduce planning to the "description" of needs is an oversimplification of the problem of the formulation of ends, the practice of staying with existing wants oversimplifies the description of the action of human desires, and "escapes" the problem of moral responsibility. The writer quoted sees clearly that social planning aims to provide for the fulfillment of the desires of people and that these are not to be confused with the "neutral" or "authoritarian" judgment by the planner as to "what they ought to want." What he does not see, however, is that there is no escaping the responsibility of choosing between wants. Any activity of providing for desires will frustrate or eliminate some, satisfy others, and create new ones.

The motive which leads to the rejection of choice among competing desires is often noble enough. It is evident in the passage just quoted. But democratic planning cannot be obtained by shunning moral responsibility. By facing up to the fact of conflict we can, if we are somewhat intelligent and quite lucky, exploit it to provide for a democratic and progressive enrichment of human life. Our first principle of planning is, then, the following: The planning enterprise must accept moral responsibility for choices among conflicting desires.

This principle might be called the doctrine of ethical pluralism.

---

[1] Adolf Berle, *New Directions in the New World* (New York: Harper & Brothers, 1940), pp. 70-71.

Although all desires may affect economic enterprise, it is plainly not true that planning can simply reduce the plurality of desires to certain economic needs and proceed to provide conditions for their satisfaction. Desires which might be classified as desires (and their opposites) for beauty, decency, self-respect, emotional communication, responsibility, etc., are bound to be affected, for better or for worse, by economic plans. Hence planners must take time from their urgent "practical responsibilities" to provide for research in, and co-ordination of, anthropological, sociological, and psychological data which will help them to fulfill this responsibility.

A crucial question which has emerged from our first principle, and which we postpone for the time, is this: How can moral control of choices be democratically instituted? Or how can such controls move in a democratic direction?

III

Successful planning must be ethical and pluralistic in its formulation of objectives and in its evaluation of the human consequences of its techniques and plans. It is equally clear that it must be pluralistic in its theory of social causation. In a time such as ours, when economic factors are so evident and pervasive and so evidently mismanaged and costly to human life and human endeavor, the theory of economic determinism readily becomes commonplace. This is a costly and fatal error. Anthropology has demonstrated beyond any reasonable doubt that non-economic factors influence economic processes. It is nothing short of thoughtless treason to the human venture to assume *a priori* that under no conditions do cultural, non-economic factors influence economic consequences in a *crucial way*. It therefore becomes the moral responsibility of the planning enterprise to watch carefully for such conditions, and to find out by continual research how such factors interact with economic factors in order that they may be *used* (not fatally neglected) in drawing up and executing means to achieve its objectives, and in formulating the objectives to be achieved.

Our second principle, accordingly, is this: The theory of pluralistic social causation must be taken seriously, employed, and continually refined in economic and social planning.

The crucial question which follows from this principle, which again we postpone, may be formulated as follows: How can choices made in planning activities (and in the activities involved in the execution of the plans) be causally controlled so as to provide data on social causation?

IV

Perhaps the most difficult concept to grasp is that of the relation between the drawing up of the plans and their execution. But the growing importance of the concept of *participation* among public administrators and planners is a hopeful sign. The difficulty issues in part from the deeply engrained traditional assumption that policy-making is a separate function from execution. There is no longer any excuse for the deliberate perpetuation of this assumption by professedly democratic planners. Unless we can envisage alternative administrative [2] (and legislative) procedures which unify the two in an ongoing democratic process, we shall rapidly "plan" ourselves (because of the failures of our plans) into the vicious social decline which accompanies dictatorial societies.

In a relatively rigid, folkway society, the wise plans of the ruling regime can be executed with a minimum of coercive power. Unwise plans are those which are made without regard to the habitual patterns of anticipations and responses of the people. What coercive power is necessary to execute wise plans, in such a society, is found to be *just* by the people; crime can be unambiguously identified for the most part and is taken to be immoral.

But our medieval folkways have been undermined by the Industrial Revolution. The rapid drift of modern industry over the face of the earth has accelerated the development of novel conditions and novel responses. The prevailing uncertainty in our an-

---

[2] For pioneering efforts in this area, see John M. Gaus, Leonard D. White, and Marshall E. Dimock, *The Frontiers of Public Administration* (University of Chicago Press, 1936).

ticipations is the basis of our various perplexing species of *insecurity;* we search for "escape from freedom." There has been no plateau of social change during which new folkways could be gradually accumulated, and our mistaken faith in fixed economic "laws" enabled us to eschew the problem of experimentally instituting cooperative, voluntary moral controls in lieu of the folkways. Accordingly, there is no social *structure* (or hierarchy of statuses and functions) to serve as the means of controlling the execution of plans. Hence the growing (and futile) use of coercive power today. There is no reason to believe that this cancerous growth will be killed by anything other than the deliberate (planned) institution of methods of executing plans.

We have seen (in our first principle) that one costly ambiguity in the concept of planning is that of the separation of the formulation of objectives from the drawing up of the plans. Both must be included in the planning enterprise. The second ambiguity, which we are now considering, is that of the separation of the execution of the plan from the planning procedure. Lacking folkways and omniscience, plans must be continually reformulated in the very process of being carried out. But they are carried out in the lives of the people whose activities are planned. Hence, except as the people are brought to *participate* in the planning, the plans cannot be successful. Planning, in other words, must incorporate as an inherent part of its activities an experimental adult educational process organized around the problem of planning.[3] The only way

---

[3] The "great books" educational program is tolerated by many as a harmless recreational indulgence. It provides the participants with the feeling that they are being "intellectual" and it gives otherwise unoccupied "intellectuals" something to do. Unfortunately, it also provides the illusion that one is being educated. In a fluid society such as ours, "great books" are at best harmless; and they can be positively harmful as reactionary forces *except* as they are read in their cultural setting for the intuitive or conceptual light they throw upon the formulation and solution of current problems. As George Geiger has observed in *Philosophy and the Social Order,* "The neo-Aristotelians are themselves doing a notable disservice to books by insisting on making them eternal and discontinuous with any particular historical setting" (Boston: Houghton Mifflin, 1947, p. 357). This book could well serve to introduce planners to the philosophical significance of their undertaking. I wish to acknowledge my indebtedness to Geiger's book, *Toward an Objective Ethics* (Yellow Springs, Ohio: Antioch Press, 1938), especially Chapter 8.

we can formulate our problems so that they lend themselves to progressive solution and reformulation (which is perhaps the core of the scientific method) is by experimental social action, in which we continually search for and refine *relevant* ideas to guide our trials. Planning experts must learn how to formulate data and techniques which are relevant to, and which can be used by, the layman. And they must accept with deep seriousness the responsibility of learning *with the layman* how data and techniques can be useful to him. It is not enough to work with and to try to help governing bodies and official planning boards. For members of these groups *execute* the plans in only one very narrow sense of the term. The plans are executed—it is worth repeating—as they are carried out in the lives of people, and they will be executed intelligently and therefore planned intelligently only as people come to share in the enterprise.

The warning has been sounded that we should expect more government interference and centralized planning. Government *interference* is, by connotation, the use of coercive measures to secure certain objectives. But, like other basic concepts, the concept (and status) of government has become fluid today. During the dismal thirties, there were a few beautiful illustrations of government "interference" which were definitely non-coercive, or at least which seemed to be moving in the direction of minimizing coercive measures. Furthermore, so-called "private" planning agencies—for example, the monopolies—make notorious use of coercive means.

Planning for social welfare, instead of for corporate profits or managerial "power" exclusively, will doubtless entail the use of coercive measures (i.e., the effective threat of legal penalties, at least) against "private" agencies which know no other meaning of "power" besides coercion.[4] This fact poses the most serious problems for planning. For in the absence of integrative folkways, it is

---

[4] It is significant that Frederick A. Hayek utterly fails to conceive of functional social control, and hence conceives all power as coercive. Yet he seems to have read at least one sentence by John Dewey in which *functional* power is identified with liberty but which Mr. Hayek insists means coercive power. See *The Road to Serfdom* (University of Chicago Press, 1944), p. 26n.

difficult to make a *just* use of coercive measures. And unless coercive power is used justly, it fails to perform its social function of achieving actual control, and, instead, breeds its own acceleration.

The totalitarian governments, being aware of this fact, try to control the moral judgments of the citizen by extreme propagandistic and even coercive measures. But *justice* is a more subtle and stubborn reality than they give credit for. Judgments about justice in specific cases are not *mere* matters of opinion but can be utterly undependable, and in a fluid society they are likely to be undependable until we discover ways of testing them and making them more dependable. Good intentions about the use of coercion are not enough. Unless coercive means actually function to decrease the appeal to coercion, they are non-functional. The *aims* they envisage are not the *ends* or consequences actually achieved. The means-end continuum is further disrupted, and social decay is intensified.

This is another way of saying that good "propaganda" means effective education; and that this, in turn, means the development and use of ideas which actually perform their function as the plans are executed. Since the function they perform is conditioned in and by the lives of people executing the plans, the test, as well as the improvement, of the ideas cannot be separated from their actual operation. Unless the dictator and his elite have some mystic, supernatural source of insight into the intimate operation of the ideas in human lives, their judgment will hardly be dependable over a very long period. The alternative to dictatorial non-functional "power" is participative, decentralized control, which can be achieved in a fluid society only by experimental efforts to maximize participation.

This is another expression of the need for enlightened experimental efforts in democratic adult education centered around a procedure of community and regional studies in which experts and research institutions help discover and provide data for the correlation of problems to be attacked. On the educational side it means that community and regional study groups should be stimulated—with leaders selected from the groups, perhaps—to study "local" economic and recreational problems. As they get to work on their own local histories or industrial, zoning, juvenile, or recreational problems, on the problems in the trade union or the co-operative, on conservation studies of the ecological relations of the environment, the need for the expert will appear quickly enough. Under such conditions, what the expert has to tell them about the co-ordination of their problems with those throughout a region and the world will be found *relevant,* and what the expert learns from them will be relevant to, and often crucial for, the co-ordination of planning problems. Social inquiry is the function of the community of experts. But only as the function of each citizen is considered to be that of an expert in the position he occupies and in the roles he plays can the subtle particularities of existence come to serve and not impede social progress.

The interdependent nature of our economic relations requires the co-ordination of problems throughout a region, a nation, and the world. This comprehensive task calls for the highest possible development and refinement of *relevant* theories in every field of inquiry. Hence, a need for highly trained and specially informed experts to advise and assist in the formulation of community and regional problems. Hence, also, the need in social inquiry of a direct concern with community and regional, as well as with world-wide, problems, to test and sharpen the relevance and dependability of the theoretical aspects of inquiry. It is coming to be realized that many local problems cannot be solved unless they are co-ordinated with problems throughout the nation and the world. But we have not begun to realize the full import of the corresponding principle that neither international nor national problems can be solved in a matrix of unsolved regional and community problems. Both of the principles require that expert methods of research be continually adapted and readapted to the progressive refinement of the people's formulation of their own problems. In any other context of social inquiry, the research specialists can hardly serve as experts for democracy or as "scientific" experts in any significant

sense of that abused term. But even if a miracle of world peace
among dictatorships could be accomplished, the moral obligation
would be felt by some to choose *no* world in preference to *one*
of such a kind.

We summarize our third principle as follows: The planning enterprise must provide for increasing participation of the citizen in
the drawing up and execution of the plans.

The corresponding question is this: How can we educate ourselves as citizens (and as prospective citizens) in critical self-
evaluation of the consequences of our actions as they affect the
formulation of the objectives and instrumentalities inherent in
successful planning?

V

Our fourth principle will emerge from our answers to the first
two questions posed above. Let us turn to them first. Although
their answers must be provided in and for each specific situation as
it arises in the planning process, we are not without a theoretical
and practical pattern to serve both as a methodological guide and
as an ethical aim which can aid the evaluation of our thought and
efforts as we try to refine and expand the pattern. I refer to an
ethical approach which has been suggested and developed by M. C.
Otto, and which he has sometimes called "Creative Bargaining." [5]
I summarize it here in skeleton form, and slanted so as to show
in what way it can unify an experimental method of social inquiry
with an ethical concern to formulate and use concepts of control for
the progressive enrichment of individual lives.

Men are creatures of wants or desires. The product of the interaction of the organism with its social environment, our wants and
aversions link us together to form various group patterns of friendship and enmity. In itself, could an isolated desire exist, it would be

---

[5] *Things and Ideals* (New York: Henry Holt, 1924), Chapter 5; *The Human
Enterprise* (New York: F. S. Crofts, 1940), Chapter 5 (see Section 7 for the steps
in the method summarized below); *Philosophy in American Education* by Brand
Blanshard, Curt J. Ducasse, Charles W. Hendel, Arthur E. Murphy, and Max Otto
(New York: Harper & Brothers, 1945), Chapter 6, especially pp. 159ff.

neither good nor bad; but the demand it made would be a right, fulfillment would be good, and frustration evil. The question of the moral ought arises out of the conflict among desires, and this conflict imposes the opportunity for choice. The traditional moralistic reduction of the ethical problem to an issue between altruistic and egoistic desires is a harmful oversimplication, especially as it sets up sacrifice as a solution. Both egoistic and altruistic desires come into conflict, and either kind can interfere with or promote resolutions of conflicts.

Unless the origin and development of desires should be rigidly "controlled" by some extraneous "omnipotent conditioner" (as for example in Huxley's *Brave New World*), desires are bound to conflict. Hence, as our first principle claims, some must give way to others, and in the conflict all will be changed somewhat. But the conflict of desires is not bad in itself, because it provides an opportunity for the enrichment of the life of desire and fulfillment. Conflict can be used for shaping *new* desires which will bring richer satisfactions to the interacting patterns of desire.

The ethical situation, we said, arises in a specific conflict. An ethical concern is the concern to find the *best* resolution of the conflict. The old controversy about the possibility of "objective" moral judgments has no more place in a scientific approach than would questions about the *possibility* of knowledge of the nucleus of the atom. The ground for the claim that, to be dependable, judgments must be based on some previously validated absolute standard was completely exploded when Riemannian geometry was actually employed in physics for the improvement of control concepts. Furthermore, the concept of the individual presupposed in debates about "moral objectivity" has lost every vestige of respectability in modern anthropological and biological inquiry. The individual is no longer conceived as an atomic entity set over against his social environment. Nor is it necessary to conceive (as in the German tradition) of some transcendent, metaphysical, and absolute principle to account for his social and cultural interdependence with other individuals. So-called "subjective" factors are recognized in modern psychology to be genuine realities as stubborn as any purely physical causal tie. Modern anthropology takes it for granted (and is beginning to realize the full import of the fact) that the individual *incorporates* cultural environment and organism in all his traits and complexes.

Accordingly, in our examination of the ethics of conflict we shall assume that there is no dependable ethical standard for deciding what is best in the specific situation. For illustrative purposes we shall say that the conflict is between two opposing parties (individuals or groups) or two opposing claims which have been concretely formulated as opposing plans or aims. We should have learned by now, in any case, that it is futile to argue over conflicting abstract moral rights or duties except as they can be incorporated in conflicting programs of action. We should have learned this from science, if not from daily life in a fluid society. With modern methods of analysis we may well be surprised at the degree of ethical insight we can gain, once we learn to take seriously concrete conflicts as the legitimate material of scientific ethics.

It will clarify the method of Creative Bargaining to contrast it with what might be called mere compromise. If A and B represent two conflicting plans respectively of two conflicting sets of interests, let C be the plan which incorporates a solution. We want to distinguish the conditions under which C is the product of compromise from those under which it is the product of Creative Bargaining.

In the case of compromise, C is preferred by the same two sets of interests which would, except for the fact of conflict, prefer their respective plans A and B. Each set feels that in accepting C a sacrifice has been made because of the obstinate nature of the opposing interests.[6]

---

[6] More explicitly, in the case of compromise the interests in A find C preferable to plan A, given the fact that plan A is in conflict with the interests in B; and the interests in B find C preferable to plan B, given the fact that plan B is in conflict with interests in A. Although as plan C is carried out it will doubtless eventually affect for better or worse the interests in A and B, nevertheless it is the same set of interests (in A) which prefers C to A-in-conflict-with-interests-B that would, except for the fact of conflict, prefer plan A; and it is the same set of interests (in B) which prefers

In Creative Bargaining, however, there is a *deliberate* effort in the negotiation to change both sets of interests (in A and in B) as plan C develops out of the negotiation. The interests which go into the judgment that C is best are not the same set of interests which previously had judged respectively A-better-than-B and B-better-than-A. The interests have lost their previous orientation around A and B respectively, and are now reoriented around C.

In the absence of dependable standards, our ethical concern leads us to search for dependable criteria of the best resolution for the specific conflict in hand. Our aim is to *transform* the situation, and the interests it incorporates, into a state of affairs in which the best resolution emerges.

Suppose that in the concrete case in hand we could bring to bear in the forthcoming decision *all* of the desires (interests) which are actually involved and which are now blocked in the situation. We could aim to do this by making clear the consequences of the various alternatives which are proposed by each side as satisfactory to it. In proportion to the clarity of articulation of the two sets of interests, the pattern of conflicting desires would be set, like a trap, ready to spring on that prospective alternative (C) which provides a release to the blocked desires (i.e., which provides a promise of satisfaction, not a sacrifice).

To the extent that deceit and error have been excluded from the expressions of desires and from the envisagement of consequences, to

---

C to B-in-conflict-with-interests-A that would, except for the fact of conflict, prefer plan B.

There are probably different kinds of *compromise*. Plan C, for example, will have an effect on the interests in A and B. Hence even in compromise there might be a deliberate aim to construct plan C so that it will make for the eventual resolution of major conflicts among the interests. But the fact that C was established in a spirit of sacrifice makes co-operative participation difficult, and without participation it is difficult to see how the plan can be *controlled* as it is carried out. The spirit of Creative Bargaining is in marked contrast with the spirit of compromise and sacrifice. Yet it can be attained even out of bitter conflict. Labor-management negotiators and social scientists (and psychologists) could perform a great service by studying and classifying around these distinctions (and refinements of them) different types of negotiation (or mediation) of conflicts, whether of industrial relations conflicts, marital disputes (e.g., pre-divorce procedures), or the negotiation of prices and priorities.

that extent the promised satisfaction achieved in Creative Bargaining has a good chance of fulfillment. In any case the acid test of success or failure of the new releasing pattern and program will be the desires which are involved in the resolution. The test has not been imposed by some external absolute or dictator. The specific "standard" is internal and unique for the situation.

In our illustration we started out, by definition, with no dependable guides. In every concrete situation there is a unique factor peculiar to that situation. But there is no more reason to believe that unique differences in social affairs are any more serious for the application of control concepts than are unique practical differences in the applications of the control concepts in the natural sciences. Every individual case of a given disease is unique. But this does not preclude the use of control concepts for analyzing and transforming the situation. So the unique nature of each specific conflict does not preclude the possibility of discovering and testing principles and techniques which can help us in the resolution of other similar conflicts. Indeed, after the manner of all experimental inquiry, we may critically observe our operating principles and techniques as they succeed or fail in guiding the resolution of succeeding concrete conflicts. In this way our principles may be continually tested, modified, and progressively made more dependable in widening areas of application. "Science" as conceived in this approach is not an ethically indifferent method of inquiry but one which aims for the *best* resolution as determined by the changing desires in the conflict situations. Although this experimental-ethical edifice has a sturdy floor in the reality of existing desires, it has no visible ceiling to the enrichment of satisfactions which can progressively ensue as the new desire patterns of release of conflict emerge into life.

Following rather closely the scheme as presented by Professor Otto, we can discover the following steps in our procedure:

(1) Clear articulation of *all* conflicting interests or desires in the situation; no attempt to whitewash or cover up the conflict or to keep desires hidden. This requires that the parties to the conflict

are willing or will become willing to use the method. In cases of bitter conflict it is interesting and important to note the conditions in the negotiations under which this mutual willingness emerges—when it does.

(2) The *intuition* of an aim, or a certain imaginative projection of a direction for resolution, upon which the blocked desires spring as a possible way out of conflict. Obviously this must suggest a promise of a better alternative than either of those in conflict, given the fact that they are in conflict. It frequently happens, according to reports of expert mediators in labor-management conflicts, that not until this point is reached in very bitter conflicts does the willingness to co-operate emerge. But when it does emerge in any type of mediation, there is no reason why it cannot be exploited as a means of adopting or promoting the method we are discussing.

(3) (a) Follow up of the suggested direction by specific plans which include its further articulation into objectives and means. Clearly the mere promise of a resolution is not adequate. The suggestion must be developed into a plan which will *work*—if the method is to succeed. That is, it must actually achieve a pattern of action and of reshaped interests which provides at least a certain minimum of satisfying consequences to the interests now involved. The chances of obtaining a dependable transformation, and the degree of satisfaction to be attained, are better in proportion to the degree of *participation* that the desires have in drawing up and in executing the plan. Hence the importance of genuine representation of the interests in the planning procedure. Genuine *representation* presupposes some degree of indirect participation by means of series of directly participating activities down the various administrative or managerial lines to include one way or another every interest which functions in carrying out the plan. Hence the need to study, refine, and broaden the new participative techniques which are employed here and there in progressive administrative and managerial agencies in government, business (at least in some co-operatives), and in the trade union.

(3) (b) The continual participative search for deficiencies in the

plan as it is executed, in order to modify and improve it as it functions.

(4) The conditions stated above are sufficient for instating within social inquiry and planning the self-corrective trait of experimental inquiry. But for the purpose of clarity we shall articulate a fourth, logical factor which pervades the three conditions mentioned. This is the formulation of ideas employed throughout the procedure in a way which will provide for the identification of their deficiencies as they are employed. In a highly developed science such as physics, this factor becomes highly complicated in abstract sets of systematically interrelated concepts. But it is to be noted that the degree of systematic interrelatedness (of implicative solidarity) is the product of the development of a science, not its prerequisite. Indeed, as late as in late-nineteenth-century physics, the abstract aim of the science was notoriously formulated by a distinguished physicist in the relatively crude terms of "the picture of a machine." The abstract concepts presupposed in the method of Creative Bargaining (e.g., concepts of the individual and society, of power and control, of interests and choice, and of causation and freedom) have been systematically related in the philosophy of John Dewey. The crucial difference between them and traditional philosophical concepts is that his provide an operational leverage which can be used to connect them *logically* with the practical ongoing social affairs of our day. Thus the social operations which they direct can serve as tests for the refinement of the concepts. Galileo's achievement in his day was the development of concepts which made operational contact with the successful practices of the artisan mechanics in the famous Venetian arsenal. Now we know that experimental transformations (not self-evident axioms or fixed principles) provide the acid test of the most abstract mathematical concepts of physics and chemistry. Dewey's is a corresponding achievement in the realm of social inquiry and control. And the method of Creative Bargaining develops and applies the concepts for the arsenal of group conflict in which some of our mediators achieve occasional astounding results in the face of all but hopeless obstacles. The results might be equally sur-

prising if some of our international negotiators would take the trouble to become familiar with some of these modest techniques and concepts.

There is no way of telling in advance how well such an experimental procedure in the social area will succeed. But simply as an operating aim it is capable of instituting unified and co-operative efforts without imposing a fixed pattern of uniform response. On the contrary, it entails a search for diversity, for novel plans and new desire patterns. In our search for democratic ideas and practices we will do well to recall and to study the definition of the ethos of science provided by a distinguished British biologist, C. H. Waddington. The ethos of science, he tells us, is "an ethos based on the recognition that one belongs to a community, but a community which requires that one should do one's damnedest to pick holes in its beliefs. I know of no other resolution of the contradiction between freedom and order which is so successful in retaining the full values of both." [7]

Within the pattern of experimental social inquiry, incorporated in our concept of planning, this ethos provides a substitute for the departed folkways, but avoids their fixed or rigid characteristics. The authority of the method of science provides both discipline and an enriched freedom for those who use it in the narrow areas where it is traditionally used. Generalized in Creative Bargaining to include an ethical concern for the progressive enrichment of the life of human desire, there is no reason why it cannot provide a disciplined control of choice along with an enhanced freedom for all who participate in the procedure. Thus it outlines the answer to our first question as to how the control of choice can be democratic. Since it is an experimental method of inquiry into social and cultural causal factors, it outlines the answer to our second question as to how human choices can be directed toward the accumulation

---

[7] *The Scientific Attitude* (New York: Penguin Books, 1941), p. 93. On the relation between freedom and authority within the method when it is generalized as an inclusive social process, see Dewey's profound article, "Science and the Future of Society," in *Intelligence in the Modern World: John Dewey's Philosophy,* edited by Joseph Ratner (New York: Modern Library, 1939), Chapter 4.

and refinement of data on social causation. We turn now to a fourth principle, and to the answer to our third question as to how we are to educate ourselves in critical self-evaluation of our actions as they affect the formulation of the objectives and instrumentalities of planning.

VI

I have emphasized the term "intuition" in the second step of the method of Creative Bargaining as it refers to the envisagement of a new aim or direction which gives promise of resolution of the conflict. This is not to make an appeal to the traditional anti-scientific method of intuition*ism*. On the contrary it emphasizes the fact that no new scientific hypotheses come into being without the use of the critical imagination. A more detailed analysis of the formulation and function of hypotheses will bring to light a fourth principle of planning which provides an outline of the answer to our third crucial question about the way to obtain critical evaluative judgments.

A hypothesis in science may be thought of as a laboratory plan for instituting some specific controlled transformation. The aim (in theoretical science) is not merely to secure a new controlled process, but, as we have seen, is to test some general theory in the effort to improve the conceptual material of science. In any case (theoretical or applied) the hypothesis, to be successful, must come out of a clearly formulated problem and must be seen as a *relevant* and possibly successful solution of the problem.

However, the distinction between problem and solution is relative. In the careful formulation of a problem, incidental hypotheses are often developed and elaborately tested. Indeed, the method of experimental science may be described as the continual formulation and reformulation of problems in such a way as to provide for progressive solutions and reformulations. Prevailing concepts in science are, of course, the only tools available for the deliberate formulation of experimental problems.

On the immediately practical or applied side of science (engineering, technology) the concern may be mainly to secure some specific control of a transformation or change. On the theoretical side (in so-called "pure" science) the specific control may be considered the incidental test of the systematic reorganization of concepts. In either case, however, the formulation of the problem in such a way as to allow of a solution is an integral part of the reflective act.

In so far as the problematic situations which arise are relevantly similar, habitual ways of formulating the problems will prove relatively adequate. More or less usual concepts employed in more or less usual ways will serve to organize materials in a way to provide a place for a working hypothesis as a candidate for the solution. But in so far as novelties enter the situation, new arrangements of concepts are necessary to select and organize data into a problem. If we will think of sets of concepts as flexible tools for organizing the problem, we can say that in proportion to the novelty of the problematic situation a new *feel* for the use of the modifying tools must be *intuited* to fit them to the novel materials. A classic and dramatic illustration is provided by Einstein's reformulation of Newtonian concepts in the problem he formulated of simplifying them into more powerful instruments of controlled inquiry.[8] In order adequately to problemize novel situations, there must be a non-conceptual sensitivity to the materials which, as it were, dissolves the rigid boundaries of traditional concepts without loss of their meanings, and precipitates them again in the form of new crystals to be employed for the new problem. It is this aspect of creative thinking which lends it its mysterious air of genius or inspiration.

Modern psychological studies of *expressive* activities, however, have thrown considerable light on this phenomenon. In the face of the terrific novelties it faces, scientific social planning cannot afford to pass by in the dark. The following articulation of these findings, for the purpose of planning, is intended merely to be suggestive of the potentialities which inhere in our fourth principle of planning. Their articulation for actual use, it seems to me, must be the

---

[8] Cf. Max Wertheimer, *Productive Thinking* (New York: Harper & Brothers, 1945), Chapter 7.

product of the co-operative study of artists, psychologists, and anthropologists working in the planning context.

John Dewey has suggested that, for the purpose of social-cultural analysis, *art* be considered as the name for all the agencies by which is effected a union of ideas and knowledge with the non-rational factors in the human make-up. Furthermore, he has clearly distinguished this integrative, cultural function of art from the misconception of art as propagandistic or didactic.[9] For our purposes, then, and in harmony with several independently formulated definitions of art, we may define it as a form of communication. (The *expressive* aspect of art can readily be analyzed as a form of communication, once the social nature of the self is recognized.) Art is the communication of *novel*, non-conceptual meanings which have not been—perhaps cannot be—conceptualized, yet which must be communicated if there is to be mutual understanding in a culture.

Since feeling and thought are not separate activities or faculties, art thus serves to promote (incidentally to its deliberate and direct aesthetic function) the *relevant* conceptualization of problems. It does this through its office of enabling the *formulations* of problems to take better account of *novel* difficulties. It formulates, aesthetically or non-conceptually, felt meanings for communication and use, so that concepts can work more sensitively and more adequately in the novel materials at hand. The non-conceptual meanings it formulates are the material by means of which the intuitive act bridges the gap between the old concepts and the new, the latter serving for the formulation of new problems. A fluid society which permits art to be treated as a *mere* recreation is in process of intellectual decay, and the "intellectuals" and academicians of that society cannot escape the process.

Hence in a culture such as ours where "thought" has become associated with technology (*means*) as something artificially separated from ethical, aesthetic, and general recreational values (*ends*), art serves the cultural function of unifying means and ends. Specifi-

---

[9] *Freedom and Culture* (New York: G. P. Putnam's Sons, 1939), p. 150; *Art as Experience* (New York: Minton, Balch, 1934), pp. 344–349.

cally this means that significant art helps to remove the artificial barriers which separate (1) science from art, (2) technology from art, (3) technology from science, and (4) work (as *mere* means) from recreation (as passive contemplation).

Psychiatrists, sociologists, and philosophers have called attention to the distressing schizophrenic pattern of responses which seems to be growing in our culture. Without integrative folkways there is no automatic means of preserving mutual dependability between ideas and actions, feelings and perceptions. And without integration —which is a name for their mutual co-operation—the individual is not a whole creature; both responsibility and enjoyment lose their relevance and meaning. Insanity becomes the fashion, and psychiatry flourishes to no avail.

Important and helpful as are these cultural warnings, they too often neglect a crucial factor which is habitually neglected in most social studies. The individual's environment is not social *and* physical: it is social-physical. There can be no adequate theory of social causation which does not incorporate a theory of physical causation. Likewise there can be no dependable refinement of social perceptions and feelings without an included refinement of physical perceptions and feelings. Hence the importance of ecological studies as providing not only a channel of indispensable information about the interactions among natural resources but also a source of indispensable moral-aesthetic refreshment without which responsible decisions, based on the integrity of the individual, cannot be reached.

It is naïve to the point of negligence for planners to fail to take these diagnoses into account. To take account of them means that the planning-educational enterprise will incorporate critical artistic activities in its plans and methods. Artists, ecologists, and critics must be employed to encourage expressive activities throughout society. And these experts must be disciplined to use their own knowledge and sensitivities, not for the purpose of imposing extraneous standards on the public, but for the purpose of helping the lay individual and the expert to cultivate critical discrimination in their own perceptive activities and of both their own creative efforts and the artistic products of others.

Our fourth principle may, then, be formulated along the following lines: Where cultural disintegration is under way, dependable ideas for social control cannot be constructed except as they also institute dependable feelings and perceptions. Hence the planning enterprise must undertake the experimental promotion of activities, which we have called art, to provide for integrative consequences as a foundation for responsible choice. As these are achieved, the gap between "scientific" or "technological" judgments and "moral" judgments closes, feelings co-operate with ideas, and all judgments become critically evaluative and progressively dependable.

This is the answer to our third question. How well we will succeed in instituting the answer is a question to be answered by time. But modern architecture and drama (and perhaps some forms of modern painting and handicraft [10]) appear to offer obvious resources for this end. And doubtless a little searching will discover powerful resources in all living art forms from music and the dance to the camera, movie, and the comic strip. Without some such culturally integrative efforts, neither the expert planner nor the layman will be able to bridge the cultural chasm between guiding ideas and consequent activities. Through the consequences of art activities, the former can become dependable guides to co-operative endeavor, and the latter will come to serve as dependable tests for the criticism and reformulation of the former. As integration occurs and discriminative sensitivity matures, we begin to realize the meaning of the claim made above that there is no visible ceiling to the enrichment of

---

[10] See Alexander Dorner, *The Way Beyond Art* (New York: Wittenborn, Schultz, 1947). On architecture and art, generally see Elizabeth Mock and J. M. Richards, *An Introduction to Modern Architecture* (New York: Penguin Books, 1947); Percival and Paul Goodman, *Communitas* (University of Chicago Press, 1947); Herbert Read, *The Grass Roots of Art* (New York: Wittenborn, Schultz, 1947); C. H. Waddington, *The Scientific Attitude* (rev. ed., 1948). The educational value of simpler forms is demonstrated in the best scientific approach to art education I have seen: Henry Schaefer-Simmern, *The Unfolding of Artistic Activity* (Berkeley: University of California Press, 1948). If the methods presented here receive the attention they deserve, their revolutionary import is sure to revitalize modern culture.

satisfactions which can progressively ensue as new desire patterns of the creative release of conflict (and aesthetic contrast) emerges in life activities. But without a growth of discriminative evaluation there can be no assurance that the solution of a conflict, which is *intuited* in the act of resolution, will move toward progressive enrichment. The best solution may itself be bad except as it is part of a general development of discriminative responses. Reality is in process of making and remaking. There is no cosmic guarantee of automatic progress. The artist in his integrity is the creative daydreamer who envisages and helps to realize the novel and enriched realities which can come to be.

7

Toward an Integrated Ethics

GEORGE R. GEIGER

Professor of Philosophy, Antioch College

THE LONESOME QUESTION "What shall I do to be saved?" is being asked again these days in strange places and with even stranger accents. The quest for individual salvation takes on various forms, expressing itself in (among other things) best-selling books of popular theology and inspirational psychology, in fully publicized religious conversions and retreats to monasteries (with the big picture magazines acting as impresario), in Hollywood mysticism and political dogmatism. In an almost literal fashion the spectrum of personal redemption is being diffused all the way from the ultraviolets to the infra-reds.

There is nothing unexpected in this; nor is there anything "wrong" about the idea of personal deliverance. In these days of armed truce and scared disillusionment, any insensitivity to individual frustration would be a sign of affectation or obtuseness. That men need finally to be saved—and saved as individuals—is not a matter of dispute. That values themselves are in a certain sense dependent upon individual sensitivity is also to be taken for granted. What is in dispute—and what cannot be taken for granted—is the question of the means and techniques for achieving "salvation." The dualism which is a major theme of this volume is to be found here as in so many other places. For the Individual has been set up as an independent entity, distinct from another entity, Society. Their relationship is seen sometimes as opposition, sometimes as co-operation; and two polar forces in human regeneration are therefore postulated—Change-from-Within *versus* Change-from-Without. Or, in Arthur Koestler's phrase, the Yogi *or* the Commissar.

This is the great divide in ethics, the disconnection which has separated alleged Individuals from an alleged Society. This is the chasm which has cut off means from ends. The point is a common-place one, not to say banal. Equally threadbare is the familiar in-sistence that interaction alone can reduce the dislocation—interaction, that is, between elements which have been persistently regarded as exclusively "individual" or "social." But prosy as such observations may be, they can be disregarded only at great risk. Without constant reiteration of the meaninglessness of both a disinfected Personality and an all-absorbing, omnivorous Society, the danger, when disil-lusion comes, of turning wholeheartedly to the Yogi or to the Com-missar is that much more real.

At the risk of oversimplification, the ethical problem can be stated, it would appear, in terms of tactics if not of strategy. Granted that it is the "individual" who finally must be saved as an individual, what are the ways of reaching him? What are the operational tech-niques which alone can move individuals—however insulated they seem to be—to do anything? Take, for example, eugenics. At least one school of contemporary biopsychology and anthropology would insist that no permanent human improvement can be effected with-out the engineering of a direct change in the germ plasm. Now, for the sake of the argument, let us assume that the eugenicists are correct; let us go still further and waive also the sociological ques-tion of the nature of this "right" kind of human being to be geneti-cally developed. What cannot be waived, however, is this: Can even eugenics as a means for human improvement act directly on the individual? Does it not, instead, demand political decision, group persuasion via education or propaganda, public manipulation of techniques and details—in short, would not the apparently im-mediate handling of the biological individual be throughout a func-tion of social change? This may be too ingenuous an illustration.

More difficult to trace would be, for example, the sociology of mystical conversion. But in any case, the problem—simple or intricate—is one of the relation of ends and means, of "individual," "psychological," "moral" ends and of "social" means.

I

The classic Greek dualism between ends and means has become without question an integral part of our culture. It has even been institutionalized as in the Christian religion and in the official systems of Western metaphysics. The Socratic and Platonic insistence that whereas physicians could make us well, only philosophers could tell whether we *ought* to be well; the perennially specious Aristotelian scission of ultimate goals from present interests; the whole Augustinian drama of the two worlds—these are in a sense the very building blocks of a great part of our ideology. To many persons today, Western civilization itself is doomed unless it keeps carefully divorced the *what* from the *how*, morals from technology.

Plausible all this may be. It is easy to say that technology is morally epicene, that it can serve (bad) totalitarians as well as (good) democrats. Even easier is it to say that the whole enterprise of science is a means to be justified only by the ends it secures. As astute and courageous a defender of scientific method as the sociologist George Lundberg can still contend that "metaphysics," which concerns ends, must be kept apart from "science," which deals only with means; and that values can be approached by the social scientist only descriptively. So persuasive is this kind of contention that when it is seriously challenged—as by instrumentalists—even sophisticated experts in philosophy, if they are charitable, profess not to understand what is being said. Yet the dichotomy between ends and means, between morals and technology, is precisely what has been challenged by the very history of scientific method itself.

A denial of the ethical significance of scientific method—for this is what is implied by the separation of instrumentalities from goals —would seem to be an improbable contradiction on whatever level of discourse it appears. For one thing, such a denial contradicts the

cultural decision which has established science as itself a prime value
in our society; that is, the scientific enterprise has been chosen deliberately as a profitable way of solving problems in certain areas
of human experience. Why such a monumental value-establishing
choice has not been understood for what it is would require some
kind of social psychoanalysis. Indeed, nothing short of an outline of
cultural history might be needed to account for the taboo modern
man has seemed to place on scientific effort, for the fear of *hubris*
which has required that science be regarded as a moral eunuch.

Any such outline or analysis would have to reckon with the fact
that scientific method—a matter of only four centuries at most—
developed in a cultural setting which was already dominated by the
concept of intrinsic value. Both philosophy and theology had con-
spired to give ethical and spiritual sanction to ideals as such. That
ideals are inseparable from techniques (perhaps the greatest lesson
science has to teach) has been obscured by the very nature of a great
part of our culture, with its roots deep in the soil of Greek philosophy
and Christian metaphysics. Indeed, the entire history of ideas, at
least since Galileo, has been involved as much in a desperate counter-
revolution as in a scientific revolution. The strategy of that counter-
revolution is clearly to divide philosophy from science and values
from technology, and so to frustrate the development of a true
humanism.

But this divisiveness is a strategy which ignores tactics. Also it
discloses other levels of contradiction in addition to the one we have
been pointing out. For the conjugate nature of ends and means is
built into human experience throughout all its layers. On the level
of common sense, the false separation of ultimate from proximate
goods, even if it bear the name of Aristotle, is easily detected, nowhere as easily as in the field of ethics itself. Men act from a host of
motives, many of them identified only with great difficulty; but that
they act in terms of long-range final causes such as Happiness,
Pleasure, Benevolence, or Duty is an idea which becomes prominent
only when such action is to be justified or rejected. A man goes to
war or joins a rebellion because his group seems to expect it of him,

or because of animal spirits and the love of excitement, or because of personal pique or boredom, or from a combination of these and other motives, many of them requiring a psychoanalyst to distinguish. He feels Patriotism or the call of the Classless Society driving him to action only when he is explaining or defending his conduct. Ultimate ends are then realized by common sense for what they often are—the most egregious form of rationalization.

On the level of logic and meaning the separability of ends from means makes as much sense as the disjunction between cause and effect. Moral consequences, like physical effects, are what they are because of the steps which have brought them about; and means, like causes, are but blind, dismembered events if they are not part of a serial process. To flit from one to the other is to do nothing less than misunderstand every argument for logical integration.

But it is on the level of scientific method itself that the artificiality of the ends-means dualism becomes most glaring. The very nature of operational techniques such as prediction-of-consequences, action-on-the-basis-of-probability, fusion of tentativeness with "certainty" (i.e., of probable error with verification)—this is all to the effect of repudiating means as "merely instrumental," and ends as "final." A "final end" can mean in science nothing but a problem solved—yet such an "end" is part of a process, of a series; it is not some reified structure or goal set up in advance. Similarly, means, as they function in scientific method, are never *only* means: They are steps in an operation, but they are also landings. They are a stained slice of some part of the formulation and verification of hypotheses.

On every level of discourse the false antithesis dividing ends from means clashes with practices which repudiate it. Yet the metaphysical tradition of intrinsic goods carefully shielded from secondary instrumentalities remains as a kind of cultural hangover, as a pseudomorph calculated to induce frustration if not downright schizophrenia. Consider, for instance, the person (or it may be a political party) who is habitually vicious, unkind, dishonest, and untrustworthy in his actions, but who deprecates these as merely means leading to a glorious result. Here is the prince of self-deceivers, whose "end"—even if it be retained with some kind of Pickwickian sincerity—will soon come to resemble his program. Conversely, one who treats others with respect, consideration, gentleness, honesty, and forbearance, but boasts that he is really using them for selfish, even outrageous, reasons, will begin to find himself bewildered by what has happened to his allegedly vicious purposes. For ends are the consequences, the upshots, the outcomes, of means, just as character, in the words of John Stuart Mill, is the way we habitually act. To act consistently badly but to have albeit a good character and heart of gold underneath is, in both meaning and worthiness, pure hokum, plausible only in Hollywood. For methods are in themselves efficacious. They produce consequences no matter what may be the profession about ends.

What is more, how can ends be honestly discriminated unless they are directly connected with the machinery for their realization? To believe in Ends-by-Themselves is at the same time to choose some pet end and to hold it obstinately, even ruthlesssly, with no possible way to justify or reject it. The believer in the superiority of a Nordic race will not appreciate Jews and Negroes. But his anti-Semitism and Negro-baiting will, of course, be "only" a means for achieving the splendid end of a society of White-Native-American-Protestants. Yet how can his honorific goal—so different, to be sure, from quotas and Jim Crow—be judged? If it is unaffected by means, then some arbitrary mystical intuition can be its only sanction. What else remains when ends are made discontinuous with means? This may be an extreme case, but the issue it presents is fundamental. A legitimate choice of end A over end B can be made only if decisive weight be given to the ways in which A is realized or realizable.

Without a continuum of ends-means there is no sense to ethics. As C. E. Ayres has demonstrated in economics, and Eduard C. Lindeman in politics and administration, the same is true in social science. There may be, in Lindeman's words, "non-empirical" as well as "procedural" values (like "equality" on the one hand, and the jury system on the other), but these are separate only in emphasis and technique: they become joined through intermediaries, failing which

they must remain sentimental or fugitive. All sane human behavior exhibits a form of "technological" continuity—i.e., one characterized by the operational fusion of instrumentalities and purposes.
Yet classical ethical theory, with its ends-means dichotomy, has been
largely resistant to such behavior. The resistance has percolated
through the entire dimension of "common sense" itself, even when
the very concept of disjunction is being starkly repudiated by practice. Clearly, the Scientific Revolution has yet to make its real impact upon great sections of contemporary thinking.

II

The Scientific Revolution has also to make its unique influence
operate on the traditional moral and political distinctions between
abstractions like Individual and Social. As indicated some pages
back, a recognition of this point is the essential theme of the present
paper, a recognition that the field of ethics has been riven by a
characteristically dogmatic clash between bloodless categories such
as Individual and Social. Two contrasting recipes for human regeneration have been placed before us. One appeals directly to the
individual. It argues that, unless man is changed first from within,
nothing can be effected. His heart must be cleansed, his inner motives
and will must dominate; institutional change will then follow as a
matter of course. The second point of view minimizes the individual
and magnifies the conditioning powers of his social environment.
Institutional change demands no inner compulsives. Man will automatically adapt his ethics to a new social order just as the chameleon
adjusts to shifting colors.

These alternatives are put as sharply as possible, and as so put
each is evidently inadequate. This is true even of the second, which
represents, although in a gross and exaggerated form, the alternative
that would be preferred in these pages. But the overstatement of that
position presents at least two major weaknesses. One is that it entirely underestimates the psychological subtleties and intricacies of
its "individual," making it no more than a monotonous register of
impersonal social manipulation. The other, much more serious, is

that it provides no method for deliberately changing the social environment. Revolutions make men, but men also make revolutions. A strictly one-way causal process from society to individual seems conspicuously futile.

Just as futile is the first of the traditional interpretations, that of regarding the moral sphere as alone one of internal motivation and subjective desire, of good will and dutiful conscience. It implies that ethical movement must be through the difficult channel of exhortation and preaching: the offices of a pilot-priest of some sort are indicated, with no course but that of inspired improvisation. Millennia of religious persuasion have demonstrated the devious route of such an introverted approach.

The alternatives, of course, have been presented too stringently. It is a bromide to point out that all conduct is a transaction between elements of human nature and their physical and cultural setting, that the moral dimension is as much a matter of interaction as the dimension of walking (in the words of John Dewey) "is an interaction of legs with a physical environment." This is not simply—in ethics or in walking—a middle-of-the-road position. Its purpose is to reduce the classic split in ethical theory. Among other things, interactionism suggests that "social" and "individual," as customarily used, may be merely abstractions having little referential significance. This would certainly be the case if the terms were thought to have a fixed meaning and an independent status, so that Society came to be regarded as an entity in itself, having its own values as over against those of the individual; and Individuality came to be understood as a prime example of splendid isolation, unmoved by what goes on without. Apparently those who take seriously the Yogi-Commissar disjunction also take seriously the rival and competing notions of Individual *versus* Society.

Yet, having said this, one must go on to say that the idea of interactionism, important as it is, should not obscure a pattern still more important. For interactionism requires that the cultural environment be credited (or debited) with providing the conditions under which individuals are formed. Environment furnishes opportunities, obligations, new claims and ideas; it is not simply the backdrop for moral character, but the very stage-setting in which the character develops and the stage on which it walks. George Mead's thesis about the Self, now being rediscovered by the inter-personal psychologists, and others, needs to be looked at again by the moralists. A naturalistic approach to the moral personality must be by way of techniques for *reaching* that personality. The fulcrum must rest upon the educational, social, conditioning devices which alone can move, develop, and even create moral individuals. It is only when we turn our backs upon the notion of a preciously in-sulated Individual with his changeless nature and his inaccessible feelings that anything like ethical control and prediction become possible. *The* Individual can be touched perhaps by metaphysics alone; *specific* individuals are moved by specific social interactions.

In other words, the concept of interactionism or transactionism would deprecate the very use of abstractions such as Individual and Society and would turn to something else. For example, *what* per-sons will be aided or harmed by this or that act? Just how will these particular persons be affected? Why are they in situations which make their being harmed or aided a problem? What will happen to *other* persons as a result of what happens to these? Questions of this type will not be easy to answer; in many cases they cannot possibly be answered with our present data. But unless this is the direction in which attention is turned, such questions can never be answered. In a complementary fashion, Society must be particularized. Since the word covers "street gangs, schools for burglary, clans, social cliques, trades unions, joint stock corporations, villages, and international alliances," it has no meaning until—like "individual"—it is localized. What social groups should perform this or that task? In what way should a specific group approach its task? What other groups will be affected? Should certain groups expand or contract their jurisdic-tion? What new groupings or regroupings are indicated? Again, these may be the most perplexing of problems. Yet they can be translated into inquiries, inquiries with content. Problems about Society never can.

The minimizing of a concept such as Society will seem of less moment to some than the minimizing of a concept such as the Individual. This will be because the latter kind of depreciation may be thought to obscure the unique and induplicable elements constituting a personality. Now, as was insisted in the opening lines of the present essay, it is no part of this argument to undervalue the moral status of the person, or to suggest that ethical problems are not focused ultimately upon some particular individual. The emphasis here, it is true, is deliberately social rather than individual (if the two can meaningfully be separated); but it is an "emphasis," not the whole picture, and it is deliberate rather than inadvertent. The traditional ethical emphasis has been too long the other way.

But to recognize ungrudgingly that the ultimate moral focus is singular and personal is not to acknowledge that the moral experience is unanalyzable and *a priori*. The experience signified by terms such as "ought" and "right" may find its ultimate referent only in the person; but there is a world of difference between interpreting that final experience as a primitive item of phenomenology—nervous and electric in quality and unamenable to analysis—and regarding it, on the other hand, as an event to be accounted for genetically and descriptively. Feelings may be induplicable and even inexpressible; yet they occupy no impregnable position, unassailable by the forces of scientific inquiry. Feelings, even of "ought" and "duty," are traceable responses; they are consequences of other events. Such a contention in no way belittles the precious and ineffable qualities of private experience; it simply insists that even an incandescent phenomenon like this is not privileged and unaccountable. The inner dimensions of the sexual experience do not preclude a Kinsey report.

It is realized, of course, that this insistence upon the accessibility of the most introverted hedonic tones to intelligent explanation (and even control) begs the whole traditional question of the descriptive *versus* the normative. Although it is evident that such an impressive disjunction cannot be handled in the present context, it must be just as evident that it is being regarded as still another aspect of the dualism which is being criticized in this chapter and in this volume. But at least one point may be proposed here on this issue of morals *versus* intelligence (an issue, by the way, which really received its definitive statement in Genesis 2:17): If the dimension of "ought" (allegedly the only genuine dimension of ethics) is indeed too elemental and primitive to be analyzed and too "phenomenological" to be made public, on what basis can judgments be judged? By what criterion are private intuitions and imperatives to be accepted or rejected? Are they simply to be taken for granted, and given a rationale and a consistency as in Sidgwick and others? This problem of choosing among judgments, of evaluating values, is so overpowering in its implications that every effort must be made to secure as much information as possible about this introverted dimension of moral norms and insights. If no reliable data become available and scientific descriptions really have no relevance for the field of ethics, that is something (a) which we should discover experimentally rather than simply rely upon the ukases of persons called philosophers; and (b) which may make us take an entirely different approach to the kind of human knowledge which, classically, has been called moral. In any event, to choose among values requires as a minimum condition that the supposedly inner realm of evaluation be at least ventilated.

If we may repeat ourselves, then: To recognize ungrudgingly that the ultimate moral focus is singular and personal is not the same thing as a recognition that the moral experience is unanalyzable.

III

This "moral person" we have been talking about is not an untouchable. True enough, a "person" is indeed separate, discrete, and alone—but only from a carefully restricted viewpoint. Is it, for example, a bundle of electricity and electromagnetic waves, of reflexes and bone and hair, which even the most incorrigible individualist has in mind when he warns us, say, against the domination of Society? The individual, in this area, is at most an interesting biological and physical specimen. But an individual is more than a specimen. He is a personality, a congeries of habits, with reflexes conditioned and operating, speaking a specific language and eating peculiar food—and loving or hating Stalin. This is what we mean by the term: Any other referent would be as unreal and as un-pleasant as William James' mechanical sweetheart. Instead of being aloof, the moral person has been the very creature of his surround-ings, and his supposedly impregnable human nature has undergone fantastic acrobatics, not simply from one millennium to another, but from war to war, treaty to treaty, and even from one ruler (or elec-tion) to the next. Moral personality *can* be turned and directed and made over—but only when it can be reached.

The bias of great sections of ethical theory is to the effect that morals is a theme by itself, and that the chief prerogative of the Individual is to gain admittance to metaphysical workshops where he will be served by a moral sense, by will and motive, by categorical imperatives and Absolute Goods. The point of the present argument is, instead, to call attention to the social phenomena which form the permanent basis for the lives that moral and immoral creatures lead. To understand those phenomena is to prepare a background for relevant ethical knowledge and to help overcome the perennial dualism between intelligence and conduct. This is no more or less than the insistence that ethical theory and social theory must work together if moral philosophy is ever to become operative, that ends and means can never function as discontinuous entities, that no divorce can be allowed between intrinsic experiences and those which are "merely" instrumental. For we cannot be content with a moral philosophy which confines itself to casuistry, dialectic, or apologetics. Moral concern must be directed rather to questions like these: How can individuals be *made* "moral"—i.e., how can they achieve expression and how can they realize their opportunities, how can they in fact *become* complete individuals, how can they *develop* integrated personalities and thus transform random and truncated experiences into consummatory experiences? What conditions will enable men to realize to the utmost their capacities for all-around growth? These questions would miss the point of ethical inquiry and be sentimental *only if they were detached from the specific and objective data which a developing science of man will be able to supply.*

An approach like this does not imply that moral philosophy should fail to concern itself with broad, general problems of human conduct. As with all philosophy, such a concern is part of the standard definition. But an interest in social affairs, in the dominating background which helps to give human conduct its perspective and direction, will suggest ways and means for making even the broadest question more relevant. For example, to become interested in the aims and methods of pre-school child training will help, not hinder, a philosopher's concern with how the "right" emotional attitudes in men and women can be secured. To know at first hand something about the details of race relations will implement rather than frustrate philosophic and religious hopes about universal brotherhood— since those hopes remain but pious mouthings without a knowledge of the hard, workaday difficulties which must be reckoned with and overcome. To confess to working in co-operative movements or in labor mediation or in political persuasion (even ringing doorbells) is also to confess that one's theories about social change and ethical reconstruction have been taken out of cold storage and put into a situation where, to some degree at least, they can be tested. In other words, if there is to be operational meaning in ethics, some experimental possibility must be presented; and it would appear that the only real opportunity for ethical experimentation lies in the development of socio-psychological, economic, and political knowledge.

But moral philosophy has often regarded itself as superior to these mundane concerns. To talk abstractly about right and wrong has been considered more significant and more philosophically elegant than to be concerned over malnutrition, terrorism, unemployment, coercion, and psychic frustration; to argue about depravity or perfectionism has seemed more profound than to investigate the conditions behind either one. As an illustration, among the most disconcerting spectacles which haunt the searcher for the good life are the mad scrambles of man to satisfy his material wants and to secure power. (Which scramble is the more compelling will depend upon one's philosophy of history and of psychic motivation.) Struggles like these seem brutish and unaesthetic to the dreamer of perfect cities; he is amazed at the exaggerated stressing of capacities for ruthless self-advancement so remote from the ideal standards of human conduct. But can these complaints against the grasping, selfish, and warlike character of human society be sympathetically received unless they are accompanied by an interest in the conditions which form or deform the structure of that society? The "materialism" and lust for power which traditional ethics attacks are indeed portentous symptoms. They are symbols of forces which have made man a rather clever, predatory animal instead of the son of the gods of whom the philosopher-poets and prophets have sung. But can "materialism" and the ruthlessness of power be moralized away? Will they yield to exhortation alone?

If philosophy can lay claim to any single characteristic, it is that of catholicity, of being devoutly interested in all phenomena. There never has been any doubt, of course, that philosophers were interested in making judgments about human conduct and in exploring the meanings of those judgments—the latter an analytical concern which at present exercises an almost hypnotic appeal upon the practitioners of philosophy. These interests, normative and analytic, are unexceptionable. What is being asked for here is an extension of the moral philosopher's traditional questions. His synoptic vision and his logical rigor do not need to be exhausted in exploring consummatory experiences alone, much as they need to be explored. Instrumentalities must also claim his attention. If not, "an integrated ethics" would turn into a meaningless jumble of words—although that itself might not be important. What is important is that all integration—logical, aesthetic, personal, to mention no other—becomes a similar jumble. It cannot survive the dualism between purposes and actions. A genuine *philosophia perennis* would seek to overcome that dualism, in ethics and in all things.

8

A Biosocial Approach to Ethics

NORMAN CAMERON

Professor of Psychology and Psychiatry, University of Wisconsin

MORAL CRITICS, if we are to believe what they say and what others say about them, exhibit a rather remarkable unanimity of opinion concerning their own times. For no matter when or where they live, we find them engaged in denouncing their contemporaries for being less wise and more irresponsible than the people belonging to a dead past. On the other hand, what records we have of human achievement—in the techniques of social agreement as well as in the techniques of industry and agriculture—seem to indicate an over-all trend in the direction of increasing wisdom and an increasing acceptance of human responsibility for human ills and human welfare. In the presence of this sharp contradiction, we may conclude either that the records of our social past have all been systematically falsified by evil agents, or that our moral critics are for the most part chronically disappointed men—perhaps made gloomy by too much devotion to the pessimistic prophesies of their disillusioned predecessors.

I

Of man's recorded achievements, one of the greatest has been the growth of mature, objective attitudes toward *environmental* conduct. Natural conditions and natural events, once treated as if they were wholly or in large part outside the proper sphere of human control, have more and more been brought within it. And once brought within it, they have been accepted by man as thenceforth his own responsibility. Thus, for example, deserts and floods are no longer regarded officially in Western civilization as, respectively, the habitation and the personification of vengeful, malicious spirits, to be placated and exorcized but never overcome.

Deserts and floods, in the course of history, have become challenges to man's improving techniques of prediction and control, to his mature assumption of human responsibility for human affairs. The flood waters which, in the face of verbal threat and verbal appeal, continued to devastate fertile country and to rush wastefully through the unfertile, have been contained through human effort—and then released in moderation to make deserts fruitful and to bring light and power to those who live in them. The great systems of flood-control dams in contemporary America symbolize the transformation of destructive environmental conduct into beneficent conduct—a transformation accomplished without a change in anything but the timing and the organization of natural events.

One thing that cannot fail to impress the modern student of morals, in witnessing achievements such as this, is the procedure by which the principles governing the control of environmental conduct are derived. For it is clear that these guiding principles of environmental conduct—these verbal, mathematical, graphic, and manipulative formulas—are derived ultimately from the observed behavior of deserts and floods, from the tested properties of water and soil. They are not the product of our cultural heritage of aphorism, poetry, and song. They owe their authority to their utility, and their utility to the faithfulness with which they represent what they are supposed to represent.

No less impressive than this is the relative ease and readiness with which man, in regulating environmental conduct, improves upon or discards his hard-won formulas when they prove ineffectual in practice or mutually contradictory. He does not, for example, mistake the guiding principles that he has derived in the science of hydrodynamics for eternal and immutable laws. If his systems of flood control, water supply, and power development fail to meet the demands that new situations create, man turns at once to re-examine his basic formulas, his guiding principles. He investigates anew the conduct and the relationships out of which his principles were originally constructed. He does not react to failure and impending disaster—as his ancestors once did—by pleading with or threatening the waters. Man no longer officially blames the rain gods or his neighbor's sins for the evil consequences of his own incompetence. He seeks enlightenment through renewed inquiry, through the evolution of new techniques and new principles, which he knows can come only from his own efforts.

Such mature extensions of human responsibility into the ancient domains of superstitious fatalism have always proceeded hand in hand with the extension of testable formulations, and therefore with the growth of scientific prediction. Whenever this threefold advance has been carried through with intelligent and humane courage, man has steadily improved his lot. He has reduced the misery and the insecurity which his previous ignorance, and his childlike dependence upon word-magic, had earned him. He has learned that, in his attempts to manipulate environmental conduct, he cannot divorce principle from practice, that he must continue to develop his techniques and his guiding formulas out of his interaction with the very environment he seeks to regulate.

II

There has probably never been a phase in the growth or decline of human culture during which curiosity and concern over the regulation of *human* conduct have been absent. The welfare and safety of peoples seem always to have depended upon internal peace and concerted action. Consequently, man seems always to have been preoccupied with the problems of securing domestic amity and co-operation, and of averting the disasters that follow the breakdown or the slow erosion of community organization. Out of the needs for conjoint agreement, for workable interpersonal relationships, for participative enterprise, and for the mutual protection of mutual rights, have been developed the verbal and manipulative principles upon which man believes the security and the strength of human communities to depend.

It seems obvious to the student of human cultures that rules of conduct, laws and customs, manners and morals, have developed for the most part in direct relation to practical difficulties. The attempts man has made to regulate human conduct have resulted in the development of human formulations, derived from human behavior in interpersonal relationships—regardless of what authority may subsequently have been imputed to such principles, in terms of some force external to human conduct. These formulations, in short, are the crystallized verbal precipitates of previous human action, interaction, and counteraction. They are generalizations, based originally upon empirical observation and interpretation, which can be transmitted in symbolic form to guide future generations in the regulation of human affairs.

Thus it is clear that adherence to culturally transmitted principles of human interrelationships has much in common with adherence to the principles of hydrodynamics which we have been discussing. Both amount to an acceptance of formulations which have worked reasonably well in the past, or which seem to promise reasonable improvement in the foreseeable future. In times of great social change, disaster, or decline, men are often forced to re-examine and revalidate the principles by which they have been regulating human conduct. They are often pushed to observe afresh and re-investigate the individual behavior and the interpersonal relationships out of which their principles were originally derived. Sometimes the survival or the transformation of a culture has been determined by the success with which some of its prescriptions and proscriptions have been amended or discarded in accordance with new, inexorable demands created by a fundamental change in the conditions of living.

One of the gravest problems that great social change presents to any human society is the one of deciding which of its ethical formulations are proving ineffectual, and what procedures shall be adopted in modifying these, or in developing new ones. In the regulation of human conduct, as in the control of environmental conduct, the validity of verbal and manipulative formulas must be determined by the faithfulness with which they represent what they are supposed to represent, and by the consequences that follow upon their application, for the individual as well as for the group. Since these verbal and manipulative formulas are derived ultimately from social behavior, their truth will come from the results of their utilization in further social behavior. When conditions change and social organization changes, the revision of old formulas and the derivation of new ones must come about through procedures similar to those by which the old ones were originally obtained— that is, through the observation of human interaction in human society.

To a considerable degree this is exactly what is happening in contemporary American life, even though some of the persons most earnestly engaged in ethical re-evaluation are often reluctant to recognize what it is that they are doing. Social organizations are accepting responsibility for human conduct more and more; they are leaving less and less to supplication, exorcism, tears, and threats of extra-mundane retribution. Because of the enormous complexity of modern American society, and because of its rapid transformations, we have developed innumerable agencies, boards, commissions, institutes, and projects whose sole reason for being lies in the hope that they will meet our current need for changing our procedures and changing our formulations, so as to keep abreast of our rapidly shifting human interrelationships. Thus, out of the activities of our modern society, we are developing new techniques and new formulations with which to cope more effectively and responsibly with our new problems and our old unsettled ones.

III

The principles by which we *individually* regulate each other's conduct, and our own, are also verbal and manipulative formulations derived from previous social behavior. They come out of human interaction and they are supposed to govern human interaction. Indeed, unless they have a current and direct application to behavior, these principles can have only historical or aesthetic value.

But even though each of us derives his working principles of human conduct from current social behavior, and applies them in current social interrelations—just as our forefathers did—we are still almost as unwilling as were our forefathers to recognize and acknowledge this social origin and social application. We still attempt to validate our formulations in terms of absolute, fixed verities—that is, in terms of truths unrelated to human contingency, truths which are by definition closed to test and reconsideration. We are afraid of the heavy personal responsibility which is at once implied the moment we admit that human behavior itself is the source of our ethical principles, and that from it new principles may yet be derived and validated.

Indeed, the practice of deriving our social formulas from the facts of social operations is not infrequently denounced as impious and invalid. The demand is sometimes voiced that we cease deriving principles of human conduct altogether—in much the same spirit that some contemporary educators would have us cease deriving physical equations, lest these lead us into destruction. Thus, even though our present moral standards have been *evolved* through human conduct, we are advised not to *continue* with this process because of its threat of continued change. Principles which were once themselves derived from human behavior are cited as though they were self-generated and axiomatic, whereas they stand always in need of support from the sound testimony of human action. The tendency, in brief, has been to insist that human action cannot possibly yield its own control, that human action must of necessity be chaotic and evil, unless it is coerced by some external force into being orderly and good.

This mistrust, this fear that human control of human conduct must lead to evil and chaos, is nowhere more widespread than in relation to problems of self-regulation. Perhaps that is the reason why our understanding of human self-regulation, self-control, as human behavior has been so long delayed. Nobody seems to doubt the efficacy of infant and childhood training in establishing an early differentiation between what is socially approved and what is socially forbidden, the rewarded and the punished, the good and the bad. But when it comes to self-control, self-criticism, and conscience, most of us ignore the role of biosocial learning and acquired self-reactions, and fall back upon the easy self-deception of traditional axioms and the aesthetic appeal of poetry and song.

IV

It is not surprising to find that some of the most important and fruitful attempts at extending scientific attitudes and methods into the realm of human conduct have been initiated by physicians working in the field of behavior pathology. To the student of natural science, pathology is always an arresting challenge—first to his understanding, and then to his ability to modify pathological developments or prevent them. Like droughts and floods, pathological human conduct often represents a threat or an impoverishment, to individuals and to society as a whole. To the physician, trained to meet situations of practical necessity, the failure of current formulas to work always demands a reconsideration, a fresh approach, a new attack. The new attack inevitably means a reinvestigation of the problems one faces and of the techniques one has been using; and this, in its turn, leads to the construction of new hypotheses, and eventually to new tests of these new hypotheses in action.

By far the most skillful and thorough reinvestigation of the pathology of human conduct, at the turn of the century, was that of psychoanalysis. This included a courageous and intelligent attempt to account for the origin and operation of ethical principles from the standpoint of the physician dealing with failure and wasted human effort. The early psychoanalysts did what the early chemists had to do. They returned to their material and carried on painstaking studies of whatever came under their observation, at the same time subjecting many of the contemporary beliefs and teachings about human nature to careful scientific scrutiny.

One of the most important contributions of psychoanalysis to problems of human conduct has been an unremitting emphasis upon the social origins of individual morality. The early psychoanalysts began with the conception of a completely amoral infant, and with this beginning they sought to derive moral conflict and guilt from the interactions of the growing infant and child with his social environment. Their basic attitudes were thus empirical and genetic. They concentrated upon the simple facts of infant activities within the family constellation, and endeavored to build up a consistent account of the development of morality out of the needs, satisfactions, frustrations, and adjustive techniques which each of us acquires in passing through infancy, childhood, and adolescence into adulthood.

V

It is no easy task, in dealing with problems of ethical conduct, to avoid the verbal and conceptual pitfalls which have trapped conventional theology and many of our modern psychological theories, leaving them with burdensome and unnecessary dichotomies—mental opposed to physical, intellectual to instinctual, material to spiritual. It is difficult to resist the temptation to follow our well-established linguistic traditions which reify the observed relationships between behavioral organizations within a human organism, and transmute the properties of such relationships into apparent entities, which may then be represented as having a quasi-independent existence. After such a transformation it is almost inevitable that the conceptual fiction, the verbal entity, will be vested with the functions of self-regulation which belong in reality to the dynamics of the human organism.

A biosocial interpretation of ethical conduct attempts to derive the control of human behavior from the systems of behavioral operations themselves. It begins where primitive theology and psychoanalysis alike began, with the amoral infant; and it follows the latter in looking for the origins of individual morality in the facts of interindividual behavior. It restricts explanation to the unitary world in which human organisms, operating in a social field, share each other's behavior and the products of their culture. In so doing, the biosocial approach makes it possible to state its problems and its conclusions in terms of social learning.

The earliest patterns of ethical behavior, as we have already pointed out, are the direct outcomes of parental training. The young child learns to react differentially to the permitted (or the good) and to the forbidden (or the bad). He learns also to develop anticipant attitudes, of the same character, from the immediate time sequence of *permitted-act-approval* and *forbidden-act-disapproval,* in this way laying the groundwork for social conscience in his own individual behavior. Here, again, the differentiation between right and wrong, good and bad, is acquired in a social situation, through direct behavioral relationships, and not in isolation or through abstract symbols.[1]

In the earliest phases of his training, the child can have no conception of the wider implications of the specific behavior he is acquiring. Nevertheless, the process of human learning—even at the infant and young-child level—inevitably includes some generalization. That is to say, attitudes and responses which an infant or young child learns originally in a specific social setting, can then be aroused also by other equivalent situations, and by interactions with persons other than a sibling, a parent, or a parent-surrogate. Thus, in being trained to fit into the domestic pattern of what is considered to be right and wrong, the child is learning to conform to the adult permissions and taboos of his own culture—unless, of course, the domestic pattern of ethical behavior is at variance with the larger cultural pattern. Indeed, as we know, the child reared in a family or a neighborhood where the prevailing mores run

---

[1] For a fuller account of the genesis of ethical attitudes, self-criticism, and conscience, in normal behavior as well as in behavior pathology, see Norman Cameron, *The Psychology of Behavior Disorders: A Biosocial Interpretation* (Boston: Houghton Mifflin, 1947), Chapters 2, 3, 4, 9, and 16.

counter to those of the wider community is likely to develop bio-socially into a "bad," "sinful," "odd," or "inadequate" child, from the point of view of the wider community.

The development of self-regulation, self-criticism, and conscience, from such a start in simple training, depends upon the child's acquiring an ability to react to his own behavior as he reacts to the behavior of other persons. This ability every normal child acquires to some degree. He learns, for example, to look at his own body, to speak about it and think about it. This he does in essentially the same way that he learns to look at, and to speak and think about, other objects and persons within the range of his responses. He learns to comment and pass judgment upon what he is doing, what he has done or will do, just as he learns to comment and pass judgment upon the activities of a parent, a sibling, a playmate, or an animal pet. The only distinctive thing about *self-reactions,* as we call these attitudes and responses toward one's own appearance and behavior, is their *focus.* They are, in short, reactions to the person who is doing the reacting.

The child learns to give unmistakable self-reactions long before he has acquired useful, consecutive speech. But the acquisition of speech brings a progressive increase in the use and the adequacy of self-reactions. Although at first the verbal comment a child makes about his appearance and performance is little more than a mimetic echo of an adult evaluation, eventually it develops into genuine self-evaluation which is aroused specifically by the child's own behavior, even in the absence of other persons. Moreover, this verbal comment will basically agree, as a rule, with the evaluation that his close associates might make if they were with him.

What a child has learned to say he can also learn to think, and to utilize privately whether he is in the presence of other persons or alone. In this way, as he grows older, the child gains skill in watching what he does, in thinking about it, in evaluating present and past performance, and in passing judgment on what he fantasies and plans. But what the student of ethics must never forget is that the techniques of self-evaluation are directly derived from interaction with other persons. They do not arise *de novo* out of nothing. Therefore, they necessarily correspond with the social evaluations that prevail in the culture or subculture surrounding the growing child. The approval and reproach which appear in a child's self-reactions to his own conduct have their origins in the approval and reproach which his elders and associates have given him in the past. If these have been always hypercritical and severe, the child's self-reactions are likely to have the same or complementary characteristics. If the evaluations of others have been chronically inconsistent and unpredictable, one is likely to find that a child's self-evaluations will be chronically unstable and unsure.

Self-regulation, or self-control as we shall call it, is by no means limited to ethical considerations. It is a form of social skill which is fundamentally the same whether we deal with manual precision, locomotor co-ordination, skillful speech, productive thinking, or moral principle. All that we mean by *self-control* is the regulation of an incipient or developing reaction by an organized self-reaction. Both the incipient (or developing) reaction and the self-reaction that regulates it arise, of course, in response to the same stimulating situation—excepting in those instances in which the incipient or developing reaction itself provides the stimulation for the regulating self-reaction. In both cases, however, we have clearly before us examples of the control of human conduct developing within human behavior itself.

Self-control may operate quite automatically and remain inaccessible to behavior analysis. Or it may operate at any level of accessibility up to and including clear evaluative formulation, or self-criticism, in words or in socially organized thinking. Self-criticism and self-control occur in relation to all kinds of behavior, from rowing a boat to selling goods or cooking a meal. When, however, these self-reactions are given in relation to ethical conduct, it is customary to group them together as *conscience*. This is especially the case when self-control or self-criticism is directed toward the regulation of one's behavior in accordance with the group mores.

VI

However great may be the surface discordance among contemporary interpretations of ethical conduct, there seems to be general agreement in *action* that what the public calls conscience—what we would define as ethical self-regulation—is not born in us fully developed, but is rather acquired by each of us through social inter-behavior. At least, this is what appears to be implied in the insistence we find that children be given early and continuous training in the mores of their culture, so that as adults they may practice self-regulation in accordance with these mores. Thus we see that it is not only the principle of infant amorality which has been adopted by even the most diverse systems of ethical belief. There is also a widespread application of the principle that human self-regulation—self-control, self-criticism, and conscience—is actually the product of individual learning in socially shared situations.

The general belief in infant amorality, and the widespread practice of ensuring moral self-regulation through social learning, have direct and significant implications for a biosocial approach to human ethics. They suggest at once the possibility of a fuller acceptance of human responsibility for the regulation of human conduct by the same general means which have been so successfully utilized in the control of environmental conduct. There we saw that guiding principles for environmental conduct were derived from observation of ongoing environmental behavior, and from the scientifically tested properties of the systems under human scrutiny. We saw, moreover, that man has learned to meet defects in his systems of environmental regulation by re-examining his verbal and manipulative formulas dispassionately, and by further investigating the conduct and the relationships from which his principles were originally derived. Thus, by taking full responsibility for his shortcomings in relation to environmental conduct, man has also come to a full realization that his regulation of environmental conduct must come about through his own efforts. It is this assumption of mature responsibility, and this development of courageous self-reliance, that need to be extended into the field of human ethics.

As long as human beings located the sources of self-regulation in a non-behavioral world, they denied themselves the possibility of ever formulating their principles of self-regulation in behavioral terms. Even when they succeeded in placing the epic of moral conflict within the individual psyche, they could not effectively unite this struggle with the facts of behavior which it was designed to explain. But with the recognition that the techniques of self-regulation develop in and are located in behavior itself, this fictitious discontinuity disappears. There is no need to account for, or to explain away, a two-world mind-body disjunction—since we need not begin by assuming such a schism to exist.

The great unsettled problems of ethical responsibility that face us—as individuals, as communities, as nations—are certainly more imminent and more real than the problems of any two-world hypothesis. In a behavioral context they give greater promise of a continuing solution. For if our ethical principles, derived as they are from problems of human behavior, can be recognized as being themselves also human behavior—and formulated by us in behavioral terms—we may come into possession of the same possibilities for the social regulation of conduct that we have already realized in relation to environmental conduct. The attitudes in the two areas of human endeavor become parallel. It is at once conceivable that our guiding principles of human conduct can be continuously improved, and that new principles can be derived, through a return to further investigation of human behavior, and fresh study of the properties of human organisms as they operate in social interaction.

This *concept of continued derivation,* like the doctrine of continued revelation, protects ethical formulation from the *rigor mortis* that must ultimately overtake the fixed, immutable rule of conduct in a world of social change. The identification of moral self-regulation as a product of social learning relates ethical problems to the great body of scientific knowledge we already have available concerning the acquisition and modification of human behavior patterns. And finally, the recognition that ethical principles may be tested and validated, through the same kind of scientific procedures by which we now test and validate our principles of environmental control, places upon man the inescapable duty of extending human responsibility to include the operations of his moral and ethical systems.

9

Religion Down to Earth

A. EUSTACE HAYDON

Professor Emeritus, History of Religions, University of Chicago

THE ROLE OF RELIGION in the drama of time clamors for clarification. Much of the cultural confusion of our modern age flows from failure to understand the central theme of the human adventure. We have lost direction and orientation. Blind devotion as well as bitter antagonism toward local and temporary embodiments of religion are wasting human powers. Priests and theologians of all cultures lavish anxious care upon the sacred vestments of cult and dogma which living religion has long outgrown.

Religions die defending their past, denying the future. Ecclesiastical housekeeping stifles the religious spirit. An authoritarian church, buttressed by dogmas of its own creation, reaches out for institutional power and wealth, trampling the fair flowers of the democratic ideal. The masters of our intellectual, aesthetic, scientific, and material resources have not been challenged to loyalty. The vast instruments of power at present shaping civilization have been used with little sense of responsibility for human values and have entirely escaped orientation in the service of the religious ideal. If religion has a claim to leadership in human affairs, it is time to understand the factual basis of the claim.

What then is religion? Because of its endless multiformity, it has been difficult to catch religion in the net of a simple, all-inclusive formula. During the last century there have been thousands of discordant definitions. The partisan was always inclined to weight the definition with the characteristics peculiar to his own religion. Sectarian bias dictated the separation of the one "true" from the many "false" religions. Secular bias growing out of sad experience dismissed all religions as "opium of the people." Definitions ranged from "belief in spiritual beings" to "morality touched with emotion." Central importance was given in turn to reason, emotion, mystical intuition, and behavior. Christianity seemed to demand interpretation as a way of *believing,* religion in the Orient as a way of *living.* Christianity separated religion from secular life, the Orient included all phases of culture in religion. Everyone knew what religion was but not enough about religions to find the thread of unity running through them all. There seemed to be no way of reconciling such conflicting definitions as "belief in God and immortality," "the conservation of values," "a sum of scruples that interfere with the free exercise of our human faculties." Some scholars gave up the quest, asserting that religion could not be defined.

During the last two decades, however, with more adequate knowledge of the history of cultures and the increasing illumination furnished by the social sciences, there is a growing consensus among the scholars in the field as to the nature of religion. The emphasis gradually shifted from what men believed, to what they did, and finally to what they were trying to attain—from the theology, to program, to values. When attention was at last centered upon the patterns of human desire seeking fulfillment, the story of religions came alive with new meaning. The myriad forms fell into perspective. Religion appeared as the thread of meaning running through the agelong human enterprise, lighting up with significance all man's cultural achievements, continuing on the human level the main motif of the planet's life—the adjustment of desire-driven organisms to environment. The families of mankind could be seen finding their separate paths through history, wrestling with the problems of nature and of human nature, seeking always the satisfying life. In innumerable embodiments, changing through the

centuries, the religious quest for the good life continued. As it was
in the beginning, it is now, and must be—as long as man shall remain the all-important interest of mankind. But the long, level
vision of history is necessary to keep the goal clearly in view. At
times sectarian walls have obscured the vision. Diverse embodiments of religion faced each other as enemies. Missionary religions
felt compelled to embark on crusades to convert the "heathen." In
some places the living stream has lost itself for a time in the desert
of dead habit. Sometimes a religion has built about itself such a hard
shell of institution that growth and adjustment to new conditions
have been impossible. The sacred organization became its tomb.
But the life-drive will not be denied. By reform or revolt, it flows
ever into new forms, leaving its outgrown embodiment as a record
of past achievement.

Viewed thus as the central theme threading the events of cultural
history, religion may be defined in various ways. We might say:

Religion is man's effort to mold a cosmic-social process in the
service of his ideal.

Religion is the resolute following of the star of hope through the
triumphs and tragedies of time.

Religion is a long adventure in learning the art of social living.

Religion is a pilgrimage through ages of hard experience in quest
of the good society.

Religion is a shared quest for the values of the good life, the agelong, groping effort of man to create the social order in which human powers may flower in joyous fulfillment.

Every religion is embodied in a threefold unity of ideal, cult, and
theology or world view. The ideal is complete human fulfillment.
It includes the values which a group approves at the time as necessary for the realization of a satisfying life. The cult consists of the
practical and ceremonial means by which the values are attained or
guaranteed. The theology or world view interprets the relation of
the extra-human environment to the value quest. The colorful variety of religions results from their differing content in ideal, cult,
and theology. Each of these three phases changes as a religion moves

through the centuries. The values of the ideal are relatively stable since they are rooted in human desires and the needs of social living. With the advance of civilization more stress falls upon social than upon material values. In eras of cultural defeat the realization of the ideal values may be postponed to a future age or projected to an afterlife or a supernal, spiritual realm. Through these changes, however, they always remain the values of complete human happiness. The cult techniques change with growing experience in meeting the problems of social living, with new powers of mastery, with better knowledge of methods for acquiring values. When the ideal is transferred from this world to another, new techniques are needed to guarantee to the individual entrance into the blissful life to come. Changes in theology result from larger understanding of the nature of the world, critical thinking about the religious heritage, intercultural contacts, political and moral crises, and deeper appreciation of the place of man in the universe. This phase of a living religion is the least stable since it constantly reflects the intellectual, political, and ethical changes in the cultural climate.

On the whole, religions tend to be conservative. Existing institutions are buttressed by authority and sanctified by time. The rule seems to be: "When it is not necessary to change, it is necessary not to change." Priests are usually defenders of vested interests. They are sometimes reformers, but the prophetic leaders of new religious orientations of culture have always been laymen. Forgetful or ignorant of past changes in their religion, responsible officials have too often confused the creed and institutions of their age with religion itself, with the result that in times of tragic social maladjustment the people were left to grope in bewilderment without guidance or direction, like sheep without a shepherd.

The place of religion in history may be most simply presented as a drama in three acts.

The first act was very long. It began in the dawn age, perhaps a million years ago, when emerging man wrestled with an untamed environment for the right to live. Many forms of life were better equipped to secure fulfillment of their desires than he. Yet he was destined to win lordship over them all. How he gained experience through success and failure during the long, unrecorded eons we may never know. Even the men of twenty and fifteen thousand years ago have left us only their bones, their tools, and their art to tell us that they were thinking, dreaming, and achieving practical skills. What they thought and hoped and dreamed we may only guess. When human societies emerged from the lost past upon the lighted stage of history a few thousand years ago, they had well learned what values were essential for satisfactory living and had a system of practical and ceremonial activities for securing and safeguarding them. With them came their friendly and helpful gods.

For a long time the values that satisfy physical desires seem to have been central in early cultures. Existence was hazardous, uncertain, and beset with dangers. Man had to master the problem of existing before he could begin to dream of living beautifully. This need explains the primary importance of food, shelter, sex satisfaction, security, and safety from dangers at the beginning of the religious story. But personal and social values were also important. Man did not win his place in the world because of physical prowess or superior armor of tooth and claw. In comparison with many other forms of animal life he was, as an individual, relatively weak and defenseless. He succeeded because he learned to practice mutual aid and co-operation with his fellows. In primary group relations, the individual, to be fully human, needed the personal values of response and recognition—friendship, affection, prestige, honor, a sense of worth. But no group ever gave these except at the price of loyalty to the common welfare. It was the necessity of living together and working together that determined the social values of religion. Uncontrolled desires driving to fulfillment could destroy the harmony of social relations. Normal human hungerings could not be denied, nor could they be given free rein. Through long experience, each people found the working arrangement by which individual desires were led to satisfaction in ways that were socially safe. It meant restraint on each person for the good of the group as a whole.

The moral codes set up warning signals at the points of danger: Don't kill, don't steal, don't lie, don't break the sex rules, don't be envious, deceitful, covetous. These negative values were necessary for ordered relations, but inadequate for a good life. Beyond them were the positive social values designated by such abstract terms as loyalty, filial piety, obedience, love, brotherhood, generosity, self-sacrifice, justice, and peace. Translated into patterns of behavior by each culture in its own way, they meant satisfying human comradeship. The desire to realize these values is not natural to man. It had to be learned by each generation through social conditioning and the learning was difficult, uneven, incomplete. Yet the vision of a harmonious social order in which individuals could find the good life together was attained thousands of years ago.

The techniques for securing values in early cultures were of three kinds—some purely practical, some a combination of practical and ceremonial, some purely ceremonial. The practical techniques channeled desires directly to fulfillment. They included the total complex of sacred customs, the funded experience of the ages in social organization, political and economic practices, and the moral code. Within the cozy enfoldment of these tried and proven ways the individual could feel secure. But many familiar events carried an aura of danger; and apprehension might attend even a time-tested, practical technique if, as in the case of agriculture, there was a long delay between the planting of the seed and the reaping of the harvest. Food was a matter of deep concern. On such occasions ceremony was needed to release emotional tension and give assurance. No farmer of the ancient world would fail to plant his field, but neither would he neglect his armory of farming rites. Practical and ceremonial activities marched together through the season. There were other times when man stood at the horizon of his knowledge and powers. Faced with frustration or awed by mystery, he could do nothing that was practically effective. Then desire flowed out in emotion-charged words and gestures—the ceremonial dance, the protective spell, magic signs, curse or prayer. By his practical program man won the values which made life possible in the beginning and richer as the centuries passed; because of his ceremonials he walked with sure step and untroubled heart past the known and imagined dangers that threatened his path, and even hoped to harness unseen powers in the service of his ideal.

Most of the gods of early religions were nature powers, kindly and helpful to man in his first faltering efforts to make a home for himself in the world. They were valuable friends, real, visible, tangible, and near at hand. Man gave them human qualities and form through the language he addressed to them. He treated them as persons and appealed to them for help. Later, under the influence of the idea of a separable soul, they were transformed into spiritual beings dwelling in the unseen world beyond nature. There they grew in stature and carried in ever larger measure responsibility for the satisfaction of human desires. Usually one god became supreme in majesty and power over the others and sometimes displaced or absorbed all lesser gods to rule the world alone. Thousands of years ago, in some cultures, the intellectuals either abandoned the limited, personal gods altogether or pushed beyond them to an impersonal, spiritual Absolute, a universal, natural Law, a Cosmic Order or Fate. Yet through all these changes the ancient confidence remained that the universe, with or without gods, spiritual or material, could be enlisted in support of man's hopes and ideals.

It would be difficult to exaggerate the far-reaching effect upon the history of religions of this idea of a separable soul. Primitive man blundered upon it, and it split the universe in two, creating all the later dualisms—supernatural-natural, soul-body, spirit-matter, heaven-earth. It made possible the continued life of the gods as spiritual beings after the nature powers from which they sprang had been drawn into the known world of familiar fact. It created the spiritual realm as the secure harbor of supreme values. It gave rise to the many theories of existence after death—eternal existence on the wheel of rebirth, resurrection, and immortality. It crowded the unseen with innumerable heavens and hells as residences for human souls. It peopled the environment of man with every imaginable form of spirit and demon capable of bringing him weal and woe. In times of cultural defeat, it invited prophet and seer to project the ideal into the spiritual world forever safe from the tribulations and ravages of time. It provided some of the most important building blocks with which theologians and metaphysicians have delighted to erect their marvelous architectonic systems. These are amazing results to flow from a primitive blunder.

But all the ancient religions were still earth-centered. The pictures of the afterlife in Mesopotamia, early Israel, Greece, and China were vague, unattractive, or frightening. Egypt and Vedic India hoped for a continuation of this life in an idealized form after death, but there was never any dispraise of life on the earth. These old cultures did not dream of abandoning the quest for a good life in a mastered world, and there were times when success seemed to beckon from the next horizon. An observer of the human drama, during the period from 5000 to 2500 B.C., as it unfolded in the Near East and in the far Orient, might have reported that man had won his long struggle with nature for the goods to satisfy his basic physical desires; that the stage was being prepared for the building of cultures to actualize the social values of the higher life. Unfortunately all man's efforts in this latter endeavor ended in failure. He succeeded fairly well in learning the behavior patterns which would yield satisfying social relations in primary groups. But how to translate these social values into a happy and successful way of living in the wider relationships of complex civilization eluded him. Instead of leading to increased enrichment of the common life, greater power, better tools, enlarged resources meant only multiplied maladjustments, the intensification of social evils. Equipped with instruments of power, human desires drove ruthlessly to selfish fulfillment. In the clash of rival interests, the conflict of group with group, class with class, nation with nation, empire with empire, culture radiant with promise came down in ruins. Maturing civilizations flowered and fell into decay and dissolution in monotonous rhythm. It is true that, in all eras, life was good for a few privileged persons, in spots, for a time. There were lighted areas of splendor set in a background dark and ominous with doom. The curtain descended on the long, first act of the drama of religion to the accompaniment of a minor chord of failure.

The second act rang the changes on the theme of frustration. Defeat dogged the footsteps of man as he climbed the heights toward nobler living. His desires outreached his practical grasp; his vision always outran his powers of achievement. Experience of high culture intensified his desire for the good life and put new emphasis upon the values of a good society. Material values were not scorned, but bread alone, or physical satisfactions alone, seemed inadequate as fulfillment of human hopes. The religious ideal pointed toward a social order in which love, justice, peace, truthfulness, and beauty would be woven into the web of human relations. Men of vision talked of a Kingdom of God, a brotherhood of man, a holy city, a community in which social values would be actualized. Yet hope was ever deferred. The human enterprise faltered before the possibility of final defeat. Stratification of classes, selfish use of power, the greed of special privilege, the inertia of vested interests, and ever-enlarged selfish desires ruined the religious dream of a shared life and perpetuated the ancient evils—poverty, exploitation, suffering, injustice, strife, and fear. Discouragement laid a chilling hand upon the buoyant, naïve confidence of an earlier age. The life-loving men of ancient times who shouted their confident challenge to earth and heaven were no more. The yea-saying attitude of the men who matched their courage against untamed nature was replaced in their descendants by resignation and ascetic caution.

The peoples explained social defeat in various ways. Sometimes there was a deep distrust of human powers, a conviction that man is too weak, too corrupt in nature, too feeble in will and intellect, to build the good world. Sometimes the world was pictured as a battlefield on which god and man pitted their strength against a vast, personal power of evil. The joy of living and the good society could never be realized in this era, since truth, goodness, and beauty were always under attack from the menacing forces of darkness. Sometimes suffering was accepted as inherent in human existence, which led to a sense of the futility of all life. Even though the eternally revolving wheel of rebirth might place the individual on the highest level of being, the best life would always be spoiled by the old, ineradicable evils. Sometimes it was thought that man had lost contact with his rooting in nature. Failure to keep his attunement to the deep, cosmic forces from which he sprang resulted in personal unhappiness and social disorder.

The feeling of failure did not descend upon the hearts and minds of the religious seers suddenly, nor did it come at the same time or under the same circumstances in all cultures. It was the end result of a slow process of disillusion, an erosion of courage by the persistent nagging of social evils. Often, however, it crystallized in a crisis of culture, a great social or national tragedy. The final effect was a "failure of nerve."

But religion is deep-rooted in desire and flowers in hope. Even in the ashes of burnt-out eras, hope did not die. Eyes of faith were turned to far horizons away from the unsatisfying present. Prophets of religion refused to accept defeat as final. As long as man lives, desire drives him toward new endeavor. Sharing the suffering of the folk, the sages rose above the disorder and discouragement of the age to proclaim confidently: "Not here, not now, but sometime, somewhere the ideal will be realized." Visions of future fulfillment compensated for factual failure. Zoroastrianism and Judaism projected their hopes to a far-off era when a divinely appointed messianic leader would appear. Then the high God would renovate the world, destroy the forces of evil, and establish the order of truth, justice, righteousness, and peace. For a time Christianity clung to the Jewish ideal of a Kingdom of God on earth, but after the collapse of the Greco-Roman civilization the final realization of perfect happiness was placed beyond the gates of death in heaven. Islam inherited the afterlife emphasis of its ideal from Christianity. Hinduism and Buddhism were disillusioned regarding both earth and heaven. Heaven might serve as a temporary way station on the way to release, but it was still infected with change. The eternal, spiritual realm of perfect bliss was beyond the human limitations of the revolving wheel of time. China faced the fact of social failure during the Chou dynasty. Civil strife, greed, injustice, and insecurity eroded the old order after the eighth century B.C. Unlike the prophets of other religions, the Chinese sages did not turn to a future era miraculously ushered in by the hand of God, or to a supernatural heaven, or to a spiritual life beyond the world of nature. They kept their eyes on the earth and sought a way of life that would restore the good society on the model of the idealized lost age of the mythical rules of the past. In an unsatisfying present they projected the ideal of the past into the future.

The transfer of the religious ideal from the present life to the future or to another world has had unfortunate effects during the last twenty-five centuries. The life of man on the earth was robbed of central importance in the religious drama. The unseen, spiritual realm had priority as the home of values, the source of truth, beauty, and goodness. Sometimes the spiritual level of being became the only worthful reality; the world and human life both in action and thought were reduced to mere illusion, a dream existence resulting from ignorance, a failure to realize the true nature of being. From this point of view, earthly existence could be no more than an unfortune episode. Thinkers advised: "Don't try to reform this world. Go beyond it. Find in the spiritual realm the perfection this world cannot give." In religions with a supreme, personal God, man's central place on the stage of time was usurped by deity. Man was branded as a sinful creature deserving only damnation. His proper attitudes were meek humility and clinging dependence on God. His effort to live up to the social code was snubbed as "mere morality"; without the gift of divine grace his noblest virtues were only "glittering vices." The idea that man might create the good world was branded as presumptuous pride. Yet the fact that God was a means to human ends could not be quite obscured. The religious myths wrote cosmic history around the theme of man's salvation. A divine purpose threaded the events of time, leading to an ultimate culmination in perfect happiness for man; or world history was an unhappy interruption of the divine creative work which will be brought to perfection after the meddling forces of evil have been destroyed. In these religions the high God was loaded with responsibility for the fulfillment of man's ideal and therefore became all-wise, all-good, and sufficiently powerful to guarantee the success of the cosmic enterprise. In cultures which had outgrown the ideal of a creating, personal God, attainment of perfect bliss depended upon realization of the unity of the individual soul with the ineffable, spiritual reality, or, as in China, upon a correct attunement with the eternal Tao, the ultimate cosmic order.

When the ideal was projected into the future, new methods were needed to guarantee to the individual a share in the world to come. The techniques of early religions were ways of securing the values of this life. They were programs of social salvation. None of the old cultures abandoned them. They continued to enfold men in their securities and to give them guidance in social relations. Whatever values men attained were mediated by them. They still were the mentors of the approved way of living, the practical and working body of the religions—the *Dharma* of India, the *Li* of China, the *Torah* in Judaism, the *Shari'a* in Islam. Adjustments and changes in the codes were made to meet new situations as the centuries passed. When the future good life was to be realized on the earth, this way of living perfected might be the mode of its attainment. When the ideal could be won only in the afterlife, the code remained as an essential, preliminary requirement on the path to the goal. Christianity, with no long primitive past to give it a practical code of living, after its break with the Torah of Israel allowed the secular realm to become divorced from religion. Buddhism and Hinduism recognized the value of the social codes for this life but drained human effort of meaning by their gospels of salvation by escape to eternal, spiritual bliss. Attainment of the good life on this otherworldly, spiritual level required extraordinary techniques—ceremonies and rituals administered by specially endowed persons, acts of divine intervention for the selection and regeneration of candidates for salvation, ascetic disciplines, Yoga practices to give assurance of realization of union with timeless reality, institutions with divine authority, scriptures interpreted as divine revelation, modes of mystical insight. Meeting the varied capacities of men, the religions provided programs of salvation by knowledge, or by works, or by faith in the grace and merit of a divine savior.

For more than two thousand years, most of the world's peoples have been distracted by a double loyalty. They faced the problem of adjustment to two worlds at once. Desires clamored for the realization of the good life on earth, while organized religion claimed priority for the spiritual realm and continued failure in culture building helped to reinforce the claim. Nevertheless religions which have cut the nerve of human effort and sapped the springs of practical idealism for centuries must bear large responsibility for man's social failure.

The spiritual world, home of the supreme and ultimate values, was always central in Christianity, but during the medieval period the secular realm was gathered into a splendid synthesis with a philosophy of life, an ideal, and a co-ordination of functions which resembled the unity of other cultures. The medieval synthesis broke up after the twelfth-century because of the stubborn refusal of the Church to come to terms with the disturbing ferments that transformed the civilization of Europe. If Christianity had been able to absorb the new forces of change as it had done in earlier centuries, if it had been able to change its world view, to develop a new practical program, to enlarge its ideals, to vitalize its moral code, to democratize its controls, to become the religion of a new and growing world—then we might have escaped the modern debacle. But all the churches made the great refusal. Culture was divided into the religious and the secular. For centuries in the Western world, every area of civilization controlling the destiny of the individual in society has been moving under its own directive with no sense of duty to a common objective, no unifying philosophy of life, no loyalty to social values, no feeling of being weighted with responsibility for the commonweal. Western man has paid a terrible price for loyalty to the spiritual world.

During the last century the religious drama has entered the third act. The scene is set once more upon the earth. Vast changes in all areas of culture have transformed the face of the world. Modern knowledge has provided deeper understanding of the nature of the universe and of the nature of man. The searchlight of history playing upon the long pilgrimage of man through time reveals in clearer perspective the meaningful episodes of the great adventure. Human hands now hold marvelous tools for the mastery of environment. Resources beyond the wildest imagination of earlier ages are available for the fulfillment of man's material needs. New methods for the control of old evils—physical, mental, and social—stand ready to serve. In this new climate, hope revives that the good life may be realized on the earth. While the old religions still dream of otherworlds, movements marching under the banner of democracy are seeking to implement the ancient religious values of justice, personal worth, equality, and brotherhood in social relations. The world has narrowed to a neighborhood. All peoples are bound together in a single bundle of life. Men of good will, masters of specialized knowledge and techniques in all cultures, now appeal to their fellows to take up the age-old task, to try once more to build the good society on the earth.

If modern man is to escape disaster, religion must be given a new embodiment. It is certain that none of the traditional religions is adequate. Their thought forms and techniques of salvation belong to a world that is no more. Even their practical codes, which remained stable through many changes in theology, are now shattered by the economic and political forces playing upon them and can no longer give guidance as a way of life nor security for the individual. It may be necessary for the old forms of religion to die that religion may live. Yet it is possible that authoritarian institutions, with vast vested interests and immense power, may remain after their religious vitality has died and their traditional religious functions have become meaningless. It may be that many religious officials will dig in their heels to retard progress toward the better through blind loyalty to an ancient good. When spiritual ideals are emptied of relevant content, institutional loyalty easily usurps the place of genuine spiritual concern. There are in all religions, however, liberal leaders who are at home intellectually and emotionally in the new age and who are seeking a way of life for man in the modern maze.

A vital religion for today will not be bound to a sacred institution. It will be the unifying, synthesizing, direction-giving force in our total culture. It will not be apart from life; it will be a way of living. The values of the ideal have long been clear enough. The basic satisfactions of physical desires—food, shelter, clothing, health, security—may now be provided in adequate measure for all men everywhere if we will it so. This material base is needed as a sure foundation upon which to build the higher life of man. Then it will be necessary to furnish the social conditioning to lure into full flowering all the potentialities of every individual, so that he may know the joy of living and be a creator of values to be shared. The old social ideal of a society in which justice and love and brotherhood and peace are translated into patterns of behavior to yield joyous and inspiring comradeship still is valid. It will serve today, as in ages past, as a bond to strengthen our efforts toward its realization. We have wasted so much of our human material that we have no way of judging what a democracy of full-orbed persons may be able to achieve in the creation of cultural beauty.

The program of modern religion will be new. It will challenge every phase of our culture to loyalty in a new synthesis. Science, philosophy, business, education, art will have a unity because all will serve the common cause. These elements of civilization are no more than instruments of culture—servants of the good life—and must find their justification at the bar of religion and morality in terms of their contribution to the commonweal. They are not autonomous—a law unto themselves. They must bow to the reason for their existence, as creations of man for the service of man. They can never be justified as instruments of special privilege of any class or group or interest. The goal of religion is the achievement of human happiness. The task, in Professor Perry's words, is "to satisfy men's needs abundantly and justly, the needs of all men everywhere, by the combined efforts and resources of all men everywhere." This means the satisfaction of man's physical needs as well as the needs of comradeship. It means the cultural need fulfilled of full personality as a bearer of the human heritage. It means meeting the needs on a world scale of all men as citizens and creators. By too much faith in gods and otherworlds and too little faith in man, this practical program of vital religion has been all too long delayed.

Science will furnish the world view and life view to give man a vivid realization of his place in the vast universe, an understanding of his rooting in the long eons of planetary developments, a feeling of at-homeness in the world and of togetherness with all his fellows everywhere. The conflicting theologies and metaphysical systems—rationalizations long drawn out of the thought forms of man's cultural childhood—will vanish away. Following the findings of science, all men in all lands will be united in a common philosophy of life which will give direction to all action and a thrilling meaning to every moment of every day.

The challenge to loyalty to a living, creative religion is imperative. There is still no sure guarantee of success in the human quest. We live in a time of turbulent, titanic forces moving without intelligent plan or control. Little men with little minds toy with powers that may result in appalling, world-wide disaster. It would be a weird kind of cosmic irony if the hundreds of thousands of years of man's climb to truth and mastery should end in a destructive inferno of physical force just at the moment when hope is swinging wide the gates of welcome into an era of limitless well-being and cultural splendor. Science, which has created the instruments that have changed the world, is a powerful servant equally willing to serve the good or evil cause. Out of suffering and death, mankind has won another chance for a better future. The religious ideal deserves the devotion of men of science and men of affairs, men of action and men of vision. With intelligence and good will directing the armory of science, it may be possible to transmute the ideal into reality. Long ago Herbert Croly said: "For the first time in human history, science is endowing a religion of human brotherhood with the materials out of which it may be possible to fashion an art and discipline of humane living." Never before were the doors of opportunity so widely opened for the children of men. Never was such an awesome responsibility placed upon us as masters of knowledge and power. Unless modern man betrays the human cause, at last he will be able to translate into actuality the age-old religious dream of a good life in a world made good.

10

The Education of Individuals

HAROLD TAYLOR

President, Sarah Lawrence College

Once gain a sense of man's enormous power and pathetic frailty,
his resistless intelligence and clinging stupidity, his tender sympathy
and refined cruelty, his possible nobility and coarseness—in a word,
hold him before the mind in the bewildering actuality of his present
being, and it is impossible to identify him with what he was before
he had become what he is.

Max Otto [1]

CONTEMPORARY MAN EXISTS IN A NEW SITUATION. He is the victim
and the master of human, non-human, and·inhuman forces. These
forces were, in the past, either unknown, controlled, or confined in
their effects to relatively small numbers of people. International
struggles were, before our time, quaint affairs, discussed in formal
language by elderly nobles and diplomats, legislated in treaties, and
fought with simple weapons by men whose business it was to perform such duties. There were clear distinctions between forces of
right and wrong. Even the barbarians could be identified. They
were the ones who, without art, culture, or moral values but with
physical energy and practical power, attacked civilizations and
destroyed them. Our new barbarians are ourselves—sometimes ap-
pearing in Germany, England, Japan, Russia, America, but nevertheless destroying civilization from the inside, just as surely as the

---

[1] *Human Enterprise*, p. 202.

barbarians who knew no science, art, or industry destroyed it from the outside.

The new situation has some obvious parts. Both religious and secular morality have sharply declined as social influence, and in their place have been put material values and the use of force by powerful men, either to seize power or to hold it when captured. With the increase in the means of holding political power, resistance movements, revolutions, and revolts have all become increasingly difficult. The new situation is one in which those who can control the army, the ministry of education, and the ministry of justice are able to destroy any resistance to authority before the resistance has a chance to form itself. We live in an age of power. Moral ideals themselves have little effect in leading men towards peaceful societies.

The economic life of a country, and its capacity to produce food, clothing, housing, and marketable products, determine the stability and the quality of national life. There has been an international increase in reverence for material goods and for the products of industry, both in those countries where they are already available, and in those which have begun to realize the power which production and material possession can give. There has been an enormous growth in the means by which information can be controlled and truth invented, by radio, press, and moving pictures, now placed at the disposal of governments and huge private businesses. The distance between the individual and those who control him has widened immeasurably. The world is in an ugly mood, tired, anxious, bitter, and unhappy. Man is now at the mercy of his own social creations. He has made his collective society and now seems to be on the point of disappearing within it. As Max Otto reminds us, we cannot identify him with what he was before he had become what he is.

Yet many of those who are now concerned with the nature and destiny of man continue to identify contemporary man with a self which he has already outgrown. Reinhold Niebuhr, Lewis Mumford, Jacques Maritain, Aldous Huxley, Gerald Heard, Evelyn Waugh, T. S. Eliot, and others who make up a dominant group of moralists and popular advocates share two views in common.

First, that man is depraved, has deserted his spiritual heritage, and by his personal wickedness and sin is on the way to his total destruction; human wickedness is the cause of our predicament. Secondly, that man's salvation lies in a moral reformation, or counter-revolution, sponsored by the church or those allied philosophically with it. These two views both emphasize the basic cause of our present crisis as a loss of faith in traditional religious values, with a consequent ascendancy of material values and philosophies of ambition and power.

On the other hand, among European intellectuals who accept the fact of moral disintegration a great deal is made of the fact that the recent history of man has destroyed not only God, but man himself. Accordingly, the most fashionable thing one can say—failing the recommendation to return to traditional religion—is that life and the universe are absurd, nauseating, and meaningless. Since man is left without God, without an orderly universe, and without reason, he is compelled to exert his personal will in the teeth of the colossal misfortune of having been born at all. He can save himself only by accepting and welcoming despair, and passing beyond it to a life of continual choice among meaningless values.

Both the neo-orthodoxy of the Niebuhr group (allied with the orthodoxy of Maritain and the neo-Thomists) and the novelties of the existentialists represent an effort to identify man with an earlier self which no longer exists. For the neo-orthodox, the self must be conceived in nineteenth-century theological terms before either the presence of sin or its removal by spiritual reformation can become philosophically valid. The cure is the traditional theological cure, salvation through the church.

What is not as often recognized is that the atheism and the radical subjectivism of Sartre and his group are also conceived on the basis of nineteenth-century theological concepts of the self. It is the loss of God which begins this philosophy. It is the necessity of atheism which provokes despair. As Sartre says, of the hero of Camus' *The Stranger,* "Man-aware-of-absurdity experiences the divine irresponsibility of one condemned to death. Everything is permitted, since God does not exist, and since each one dies."

Even the existentialist cure is like the neo-orthodox cure. It is to take the Protestant salvation of grace through deeds, except that the prerequisite is different. It is necessary first to pass the tests of the theological sophistication of the atheist, and the political sophistication of the cynic.

The contemporary situation of events and societies, to which the neo-orthodox and the existentialist are both referring, is a real situation, whose effect upon modern man is of the kind which produces a nihilism of all values and an anxious search for positive security. The analysis of social conditions and of spiritual disintegration is usually profound in both groups of writers. However, the conception of human nature and of the self upon which both philosophies are based is extraordinarily old-fashioned for the support of a contemporary philosophy. The self, as we know it in non-theological terms, is not a soul to be saved or an entity loose in a meaningless universe. The self both creates that universe and is created by it. It can make the universe meaningless if, in view of wars, murders, revolutions, and crisis, we become convinced that life is merely a journey to annihilation. This is not to say that life is meaningless, but only that, under certain conditions of stress and crisis, individuals give up their belief in the possibility of progress, objective values, and even truth itself.

It is true that our certainties have all become suspect. We are no longer sure, as we once were, that the continuing and frightening tensions among countries, and between groups within each country, can be smoothed away with time and constructive effort. The inner tensions of life in cities, where we all hurry anxiously to do the things we feel we must, are working out an inner drama similar in pattern to the outer drama of the world. The same anxieties, guilts, conflicts, and inner insecurities which plague each one of us plague the world, and we find the world's tension reflected in ourselves and our own tensions projected into the world. We have constant nagging doubts that peace and security will not be achieved within the foreseeable future. We in America look at the fate of Europe and its physical and spiritual destruction as a sign of what might happen to us.

It is important, therefore, to consider not only that the physical, social, and psychological conditions for living have altered radically in our age, but that the modern self has become different. If man is a victim of contemporary circumstance, and a creature of his own society, it is also true that he has become more conscious of the world and of his circumstances than ever before. With the spread of literacy, and with the devices of mass communication, men and women everywhere have come to understand the way in which their position in society is determined for them by others. Men of every country have learned the meaning of social organization and the use of collective power, through trade unions and political movements, to obtain for themselves the rights and privileges of a material security which was formerly the monopoly of a very few people. This has meant a genuine shift of power, from those who formerly controlled all of us without our knowing it, to those whom we help to keep in power because we believe they serve our common interest. In the present transition stage, where the shift of power is still in motion, we of the Western democracies are confused as to how we can choose the leaders and the ideas which can help to achieve a stable society with personal freedom and personal security for everyone in it.

To decide these matters, we used to believe that we knew where our moral values lay, and that we needed to do no more than to consult our private judgment to determine a course of action. But the modern self we consult is more complicated than this. It is more self-conscious than its nineteenth-century counterpart. It can understand the reasons underlying itself; it can point to social conditions, family circumstance, psychological and social conditioning, complexes, and unconscious desires, to explain why it is the kind of self it is. This has tended to make it more uncertain in its judgments, and has made it seek the security of standard opinions, mass attitudes, and the trustworthy judgments of experts—or, ultimately, to seek security in dogmatic faith, either secular or religious.

But even in dogma, the self is driven back and inward, and each one of us, in or out of churches or parties, is constantly faced with the fact that it is only by our individual judgments, by our individual beliefs—it is only by the fact that we think, act, and believe individually and personally—that our own destinies are decided. There is no escape from intellectual responsibility in any quarter, since in the dogmas of politics and religion, changes occur with the flow of contemporary events.

Yet, as we consider the two major recommendations of contemporary Western philosophers—to accept traditional religious faith, or to accept the absurdity of the world—the future of man is being decided by political movements, men, and governments that, in using ideals and concepts as political instruments, move us towards a time of universal political control or complete destruction. To avoid either control or destruction, the Western democracies must work out the form of a new philosophy which accepts the facts of power, and the reality of political action, accepts human nature as part of a growing and changing universe, has a clear image of contemporary man, and meets squarely the challenge of all those who are trying to control the individual. Against the total power of a thoughtless world, those of us who are without material power have only the moral values and the sustained intellectual effort of interested people to use as our weapons.

There is no other way of putting such a philosophy into effect than to teach it in an educational system. It is true that education cannot control the events of the future. No single social agency is capable of that responsibility. But education can establish a set of ideals, values, and attitudes in American life. These can help to shape the future actions of American citizens in situations where the citizens' decisions about human ideals and their consequence are of crucial importance. In the educational system of this country are reflected the realities and hopes of American society. The reflection therefore shows us coarse, material values held by teachers, administrators, parents, and pupils, who, among them, wish to use education for private gain in moving upwards in a social and economic system. Side by side with these material aims are the ideals and principles of those who wish, by means of our schools and colleges, to change society to a happier image of what life can be.

The reflection also shows us the existence of the philosophies of education which correspond to the thinking of people outside the academies. Since the trend of that thinking is toward a greater control of individuals, toward the revival of religion as a philosophical salvation, and toward the revival of authority as a source for truth, education has been infused with a philosophy of control. Reforms in our universities are moving in that direction, and the individual, even in the environment of the intellect, has been s bject to the same pressures for standard thinking as the individual outside the academies.

At the same time, there is greater realization than ever before that the universities and schools have duties and responsibilities in these matters, not only for training the intellect, but for developing moral values. Education is now called upon to replace the home, the church, and the family. Educators are asking serious questions about the way in which education can shift the movement of social change in a direction more in keeping with the nobility of human ideals and the freedom of individuals. The report of the President's Commission on Higher Education centers its thinking and its proposals upon the fact that education is an instrument of social transition, and that the primary task of our colleges and universities is to transform the intellectual, moral, and social values of American youth so that the education they receive will be put to use, not merely for private gain and individual success, but for the development of a free community, here and abroad.

It is here that the philosophy and insight of Max Otto cut most deeply into the contemporary problem. To transform contemporary values in ways most adequate for the future development of a democratic society, it is essential to understand human nature in terms of a philosophy of naturalism. Until we recognize human nature in its concrete reality, until we accept the modern self as an individual thinking organism tangled in a web of social relations, we cannot begin to educate modern man to face the spiritual and social crisis in which he has become involved. Any other mode of thought than the empirical falsifies to some degree both the crisis and its solution. Ultimately, the task for all of us at work in education, whether as intellectuals or as citizens, is, as Max Otto says, "the enlistment of individuals, communities, and peoples, in designing and applying the most richly satisfying experience of living which human powers and the conditions of finite existence can be made to yield." [2] Max Otto has taught all of us who have been near him three basic values and truths upon which his own philosophy and life can be said to rest—that intelligence is of a diversity of types, found and expressed in a diversity of ways, each valuable and significant; that abstractions are only as useful as the aid they provide in pointing to a reality found in common experience; that truth and value are tested by human action in human situations, and not in the *a priori* or in the logic of rationalism. These elements of Max Otto's philosophy have been expressed so clearly and so persuasively in his work as a teacher and a writer that they have become part of the tradition of his university, and part of the thinking and acting of hundreds of his students. To work with Max Otto as a teacher is to discover the resources which lie, not only in his philosophy and in him as a person, but in students themselves, whose insights and ideas spring to life under proper care. Max Otto has succeeded, as only the great teachers can succeed, in creating around himself, his students, and his colleagues the atmosphere of creative thought.

It is with Max Otto's own insight into the task for contemporary man and for the contemporary teacher that I wish to deal. It is characteristic that there is no full-blown educational system developed here, but rather a statement of principle and aim for the citizen, inside or outside of the universities. Otto's faith lies in the intellectual and moral resources of common people, whose attitudes and talents he unfailingly accepts as valuable, rich, and potentially great, if only the opportunity and encouragement be given to them. It is this faith which turned his attention constantly to the individual

---

[2] *Faith, Ideas, and the Job* (New York: New School for Social Research, 1949), p. 8.

student in his classes, and to the individual human being as a citizen.

In the reform of education and of society, Max Otto therefore conceives the student and the citizen as the center of action and intelligence around which the school or society moves, and thinks of the scholarship and research of the teacher as the development of a body of knowledge which can be understood and used by the student and the citizen in the conduct of his life. Such knowledge is to be valued, not simply for itself as knowledge or as pure cultural value, but for the quality of life which it makes possible in those who have absorbed it. Therefore, the entire program of education must be one which relates itself to the student, and enlists his loyalties and enthusiasms in the transmission of the liberal values upon which civilization is based.

In the light of this conception, the approach of education to the situations created in contemporary life must be of a special kind. It cannot adopt the misconception of the nature of man proposed by Niebuhr, nor can it accept the alternative proposal that there is no human nature, and that life should move through despair to a salvation beyond it. We shall have to wait a little longer for M. Sartre's description of an educational system which prepares us for a meaningless life through the disciplines of desperation. For Niebuhr or for Sartre, the implication for our work in teaching the young is that the values must be either dogmatic and absolute or subjective and meaningless. These two attitudes do not exhaust the alternatives. American education, however, has begun to act as if they did. There is already a common conception of the means by which education can meet the demands of a new age—by defeating the intellectual forces of relativism. Moral values, it is argued, are part of the tradition of Western civilization, deriving from classical and Christian sources, and are set down in the works of literature and philosophy. The values are intrinsic. They exist in each age as elements of a rational universe, expressed now in one form, now in another, by men of vision who grasp the essential truths and transmit them to us through their work. Therefore, the means by

THE EDUCATION OF INDIVIDUALS

which we can meet our present spiritual and moral crisis lie in the provision of a curriculum for American youth in which the tradition of Western culture will be studied through the reading and discussion of the works of great writers in the history of the West.

There is an accompanying argument which strengthens this view and provides another premise for the philosophy of present reforms. It is that our students have become too specialized in their educational training, that professional studies have narrowed the scope of education until we find ourselves educating technicians in science and the professions, rather than men of good will who are broadly developed in knowledge. What is lacking is a conception of moral value which can be grasped by our students. Therefore, a program of study in the humanities must be provided for each student, along with a curriculum in other studies. In the most rigorously organized of these programs, a serious effort is made to cover the academic materials of each of the four major areas of knowledge. The term most commonly used to describe the reform is that of "general education," or, alternatively, "the core curriculum."

These arguments are clear, straightforward, and, as far as the effects upon educational reform are concerned, conclusive. They have been accepted by most educators in their work on college curriculum committees, and the acceptance has resulted in a series of alterations throughout the whole system of higher education in America.

However, if we begin, as Max Otto suggests, with the presupposition that moral values are not intrinsic, but rather modes of intellectual, emotional, and social behavior which develop in young people through the example and guidance of their teachers, we very quickly drop the notion that the present reforms of subject matter of higher learning are adequate to meet our present situation. It is true that the cultural history of Western civilization is an important segment of knowledge for contemporary students. It is also true that we have a system of education which develops narrowly trained specialists, without aesthetic or social interests. But it is doubtful that any reform which centers itself on materials of study to be presented to all students can correct the difficulties in the present system. This, it seems to me, is a misconception about the meaning of general education.

It is assumed that special education consists in working as hard as one can at one special body of subject matter, narrowly defined and strictly organized; to be a specialist in this sense is to be narrowly educated. The antidote proposed is to provide more study in other organized fields and to produce a general education, a common body of knowledge, and a common set of values for the American student body. This has very little to do with the problem of specialism, or with questions of moral and cultural value. The aim of the American student is to pass his examinations, take the university degree, and get to work. If he wants to be an engineer, a doctor, a businessman, or a physical educator, he tries very hard to pass his examinations well in the field of his choice, and if he is very serious about his vocation, he also tries to obtain high marks in all other subjects for the sake of his record. If he wants to be a teacher, he shows the same attitude to his studies, whether they are called special or general. He will study special *or* general subjects hard enough to cope with the demands he makes upon himself, and the demands the examiner is likely to make. His energies for study are wisely distributed over special and general education, with similar techniques for covering the ground in each field.

The question of general education is not a question of installing a larger number of required studies. Nor is special education necessarily narrow. It is not a question of subjects at all. It is a matter of the individual student and the way in which he takes the material of knowledge and uses it in his life. We are concerned here not with men and women who can say to the contemporary world that they have taken general-education courses and that they know something about natural science, social science, the arts, and the humanities. I doubt very much if anyone in the contemporary world is interested. We are concerned with men and women who think and act intelligently, freshly, courageously, and maturely. We want our college graduates to carry on the liberal spirit of our cultural tradition. We want most of all to have them display personal qualities which make their company enjoyable, their work interesting, and their lives socially useful. We also want each one to be different, we want to break up the pattern of uniformity which contemporary life is forcing upon us.

Therefore we must return to the individual student, and consider what kind of person he now is, and how we can set about developing in him the knowledge and the values necessary for an independent life in an insecure world. In this case, knowledge and the materials of learning become media through which his individual development goes.

The varieties of knowledge and the ways of knowing will vary from student to student, and the ideal education will make of the school or college an institution adapted to the needs of the individual student. This is not to say that the student will taste quickly the content of each area of knowledge in an effort to find a congenial subject, but that each student will involve himself in the process of his own intellectual development, at the point of greatest significance for the knowledge he already has and the interests which already engage him. The greatest total development of the individual occurs when we build upon the central value system of the person who learns—not when we take a punitive attitude toward the student who, wishing to learn more about the items in his own personal agenda, disregards or overcomes the obstacles put in his way by the curriculum, but when we pay due regard to the commitment the student makes to the study of those matters which are significant for him.

To replace the concept of an inclusive knowledge, common to all, we must set down the principle of individual growth towards intellectual and moral maturity. In this case, total concern with the sequence and content of specific knowledge gives way to a concern for the organic development of a point of view and a maturity of the self. This principle requires that the college build its curriculum and its policies upon the fact that every human being has to learn how to put together in a meaningful pattern the isolated phenomena of the contemporary world. The chief weakness in our present system of higher education is that it rests upon the opposite principle—that is, the notion that there is a pattern of knowledge in existence, contained in textbooks, lectures, and faculty bodies, which furnishes the coherence of the world ready-made. It is the practice of universities therefore to communicate that over-all pattern, piece by piece, through the medium of the lecture system and the core curriculum. This assumes that learning is intellectual perception of the kind described in faculty psychology, where something is learned if it is perceived by the reason and stored in the memory. A more accurate account of learning would show that it is a process by which concepts, ideas, objects, feelings, emotions, and attitudes become part of the total human being, and that a meaningful pattern of knowledge is slowly created by the efforts of the individual to relate himself to his world.

This process begins in the infant when he is attracted by bright colors, pleasant sounds, affectionate hands, warm bodies, and is repelled and frightened by loud noises, harsh voices, cold, intense heat, and sudden movement. In the beginning of the life of the infant, there is only the stirring of consciousness, which gradually relates itself to objects, and the internal life begins to form itself in consonance with the outer world of people and things. Both inner and outer world grow together until a pattern of personality and knowledge is established, more or less adequate for living, depending upon the opportunity provided for the growing self to become involved slowly in an order of reality. There is no reason to believe that this process, so clearly discernible in the infant and the child, is not the same process which we refer to when we speak of the higher learning. There are research data in abundance from the psychologist to substantiate it. When we make institutions for learning, the first essential is to recognize the factors in intellectual growth for what they are—stages in a total development of the individual—and to arrange matters so that these stages can be reached and passed as successfully as possible.

The next essential is to free the institution of the idea that intellectual training, the development of the mind, is an enterprise to be carried on as if the mind were a muscle to be trained by continuous and difficult exercise. The effort to learn does, of course, present difficulties and obstacles. One of the most significant evidences of maturity in the individual is the ability to begin a difficult learning task and to carry it through to its conclusion. But the mind is not strengthened by the continuous necessity of driving through the subject matter of a curriculum. The strength of the mind is increased only when the content of knowledge is accepted as an integral part of the life of the individual who learns. The strength comes from the involvement of the student in learning, and the increase in the ability of the student to assimilate fact and value into a meaningful pattern. Most students in college can push through hundreds of pages of required reading, and can perform the duties required of them for examination purposes, since by doing so, they reach a goal external to the knowledge itself—that of meeting the college requirements and receiving the reward of a degree. But the thinking, acting, conscious self is likely to remain untouched in the process. It is with the transformation of the self that all education must be concerned.

It is here that a great many confusions arise over the philosophy of the progressives in education. Once the proposition has been stated that knowledge is made by the individual, and that therefore institutions of learning must occupy themselves with the way in which individuals can put together a body of knowledge appropriate to the needs and interests of each learning person, the rationalists rise in a body to accuse the progressives of creating a self-centered universe and a society of ignorant individualists. Actually the proposal of the modern educator is that we accept the realities of learning, and that we stop behaving as if the motivation and the emotional response of the student were irrelevant to the total body of knowledge created by him. It is often assumed that to concern oneself with the interests and needs of the student, as he himself realizes them, is to pander to his weaknesses and to encourage him to indulge in indolent studies, chosen for convenience. The proposal is quite the reverse. Briefly, it is that we must discover the varieties of capacity within each person. We must ask ourselves: How can these capacities be developed to their greatest height, and how can individual talent be placed at the service of civilization? Until we ask these questions, we go on with education as if they had already been answered, and assume that there is one set of answers suited to everyone.

What the teacher needs, therefore, to move at ease in his own age with its unique educational problems, is a vivid sense of the personal reality in which each of his students is involved. This reality is composed partly of the folklore of the student's society, partly of the moral values of his family and institutional life, partly of a body of knowledge assembled from many sources in his personal history, and partly of the implicit body of assumptions which are the intellectual habits of the Western world. To educate the student is to help him to make a coherent pattern of the series of vaguely formed values and ideas he has thus inherited, and to bring to him the gift of past and present knowledge of which he is necessarily ignorant. In doing so, the teacher will aid the young to reach some understanding of their place in the modern world. That world will not be an existentialist absurdity, nor an arena for the fight of souls against sins. It will be a world in which it is discovered that human beings make their own way, slowly and painfully, in the bewildering actuality of their present being, with intelligence and stupidity, nobility and coarseness, generosity and cruelty, towards a variety of goals more or less clearly perceived. Whatever those goals may be, there is a way of determining their ultimate value for society and the individual: Does their realization provide the most richly satisfying experience of living which human powers and the conditions of finite existence can be made to yield? This is what Max Otto has taught. It gives his philosophy and his life a coherence, a humanity, and a moral quality which affirm a belief in the possibilities of man at a time when the difficulties of man's present existence have distracted the world.

I I

The Integration of Industrial Society

C. E. AYRES

Professor of Economics, University of Texas

IN SPITE OF SURFACE INDICATIONS to the contrary, I am convinced that industrial society is now achieving a sort of integration the importance of which is so great that any estimate of it is bound to seem wildly exaggerated. One can say of it very simply that it has never happened before. But this gives no gauge of the importance of what is happening now. Or one can simply point to what is happening. But an event provides no index to its own significance. It may not even be recognized as an event.

That is true of the present event. It is not to be found in any roster of current events. Nevertheless I believe that the general acceptance of the conception of "full production"—not merely by students of economics, but by businessmen everywhere and by business agencies such as the industrial institutes, the United States Chamber of Commerce, and even the National Association of Manufacturers—as the criterion of economic health and the general welfare, is an event of profound historical importance. I shall offer no evidence that the concept of full production is in fact now generally accepted. The reader has only to leaf through the pages of the papers and magazines that lie nearest him, taking note especially of the institutional advertising that has become such a large ingredient of our national literary diet, to assure himself that the phrase "full production" is indeed on everybody's lips.

To be sure, this means only that "full production" has become a slogan. Such a slogan must be taken with reservations. Not everybody who cries, "Lord! Lord!" is worthy to enter the kingdom of heaven. Moreover, the cautious reader will notice that in the pronouncements of the business community "full production" is invariably coupled with "free private enterprise" in such a way as to raise considerable doubt whether or not any of the leopard's spots have really changed. He may even venture to question whether such phrases really mean much of anything to people who so obviously use them with the intention of creating sentiment favorable to themselves. After all, he may ask, has anybody ever opposed full production?

Such misgivings are fully justified, and I assure the reader that I share them. It is true that the business community has never concertedly opposed full production or advocated scarcity, and that no pentecostal conversion to previously despised doctrines has taken place. The fact is rather that in the past nobody gave the matter any thought at all, one way or the other. Indeed, that is what makes the present event significant.

From its beginning in early modern times, industrial society has done business on the basis of a dualism. The industrial economy presents two aspects to even the most casual observer. On one side it appears to be a vast assembly of men working with tools and machines to produce physical objects of all sorts and sizes. On the other side it presents the appearance of a tremendously formidable and intricate organization in which various types and classes of individuals exercise various types of authority and dominance while others behave with corresponding subservience and submission.

The distinction between these two aspects of the industrial economy has never been regarded as a metaphysical one—that is, no one has ever asserted that one is the "reality" of which the other is the "mere appearance." The distinction has been rather one of

causal potency. I suspect that these two types of dualism have much in common, and that we always mean by "reality" those entities (whatever they are) which really "make a difference" to the true course of events, as distinguished from those which only seem to make a difference to what only seems to be the course of events. Furthermore, I suspect that the dualistic habit of thought, which has been so deeply ingrained in human mentality throughout the past, has always been based on a division of attention between the common, ordinary, and vulgar actualities of day-to-day experience and the fascinating fictions with which all societies have sought to divert themselves.

At all events, modern Western society has been amazingly successful in diverting its attention from the vulgar actualities of craft and artisanship to the fascinating fictions of finance. Three sets of circumstances have contributed to this achievement. These too, I think, have their analogues in the history of older dualisms; but I am here concerned only with economic dualism and its possible resolution.

First and most important is ignorance. As we now look back upon the growth of the industrial economy and the expansion of Western society during the past half-dozen centuries, it appears quite obvious that this whole process has been a consequence of the progress of science and technology. This is what educated people say with virtual unanimity whenever such a question is raised in general terms and outside the purlieus of economic controversy and business interest. Everything we know about the history of Western civilization (always excepting the ideological traditions of political economy) is consonant with such a view. If the conceptual framework of our thinking were perpetually and automatically renewed, that is the view it would now take. But unfortunately such is not the case. A society—like an individual, perhaps—forms its impression of itself early in life; and at the time when Western society attained self-consciousness, no basis existed for such understanding of the significance of science and technology as is general and commonplace today, or even for recognition of the existence of such a factor.

True, discoveries and inventions which we now recognize to have been among the most important events of modern history were actually made at what we now recognize to have been the dawn of modern civilization. But their germinal, or dynamic, character was not recognized as such. Even today, with science in general, and technology as a whole, as fully accredited as they are, the particular incidents which, so to speak, set this cultural chain reaction going are by no means completely known or generally understood. For the germs of science and technology to have been identified before modern science had been born—and when the very conception of technology would have been unintelligble—was, of course, impossible.

This vacuum required to be filled. Earlier generations lacked modern knowledge. But they were not incurious or unreflective. Even in early modern times, men were well aware that revolutionary changes were taking place in the structure of society. Towns were coming to dominate the countryside, and merchants and money-lenders were supplanting nobles and bishops at the right hand of sovereign power. Beyond question, circumstances such as these must be recognized as a second factor scarcely less important than the limitations just mentioned in the formation of the ethos of commercial society.

But here also what is most important is the shaping of men's thoughts. Because there is an obvious connection between the power exercised by moneyed men in modern Western society and the commercialization of the soul of our society, some people jump to the conclusion 'that our commercial masters have deliberately corrupted us. This hypothesis has a double attraction. It is easy to understand, and it points to an equally simple resolution. If that is all that is the matter, then all our troubles would be resolved by liquidating the villains who have cheated us. But, as we ought to know by now, societies are not deceived; they deceive themselves. In particular, they deceive themselves about themselves. In discussing man's inveterate disposition to invent legends which people the world with demons and impute mystic powers to every

stick and stone, philosophers have made much of ignorance—just as I have done in this connection—and also of the same persistent curiosity and attempted rationality which I have postulated. Doubtless the situation in which men found themselves in early modern times was an immemorial one. Indeed, at this point also I am moved to wonder if the economic dualism from which we are now trying to extricate ourselves does not run true to ancient type. Is the central mystery of the universe that of thunder and lightning, eclipse, and tidal wave? Or is it the mystery of the sway men somehow exercise over one another?

It is most significant, I think, that during a revolutionary period such as this men should have been as preoccupied as they were with the nature and sources of political power and the genesis of organized society. How and why do feral men institute a civilized community? Why do they recognize authority? Today we know that such questions do not make sense. Present-day culture and present-day authority derive from the past and are continuous with an experience that extends over hundreds of thousands of years. The present species of man never has been feral. Social organization actually antedates *homo sapiens*. But what is known to us was not known to any earlier community; and in their efforts to answer unanswerable—and therefore fascinating—questions, our ancestors necessarily made use of whatever their social experience afforded. They made myths, tracing the descent of their actual prince from the all-fructifying sun and imputing to him powers suitable to his actual station and consonant with his fictitious origin.

The age of reason, in which our commercial society reached maturity, had freed itself from such obvious conceits. But it had not freed itself from trying to answer unanswerable questions, nor from the necessity of deriving the answers from present experience. Since the way of life of even early modern Europe was beyond question an immensely successful expedient, it seemed obvious that a creature gifted with the faculty of reason must recognize it as such and therefore prefer it to an existence that would otherwise, seemingly, be solitary, poor, nasty, brutish, and short; and since

present experience showed that the way men arrived at such de-cisions was by execution of some sort of contractual instrument through some sort of parliamentary procedure, it seemed obvious that that was how organized society had originated.

By the same reasoning it seemed equally clear that it was the procedures of commerce and the powers of finance that "made possible" the unique opulence of the modern Western world. The time will come when our descendants will find it hard to realize that for several centuries Western society was so preoccupied with the mysteries of trade and the powers of ownership that, generally speaking, it occurred to nobody to wonder by what physical process the articles of commerce came into existence; but there can never be any doubt as to why such an obsession supervened. Western so-ciety has glorified commerce and finance because it has been domi-nated in fact by traders and financiers; and its glorification has taken the immemorial form of imputing to its "leaders" the powers, whatever they may be, that "make possible" all that has occurred, whatever it is.

To be sure, such an obsession calls for systematic rationalization. Although the commercialization of Western society was a conse-quence of the facts of modern life, still the facts of life do not ex-plain themselves. "The spirit of modern capitalism," as it has been called, could not have permeated all the levels of the community, and could not have persisted for centuries, as it has done, merely in consequence of some deliberate conspiracy of propaganda and indoctrination. But it is no less true that, to be effective, such an ethos must receive systematic formulation.

This indispensable service was performed by political economy, the third circumstance to which our economic dualism must be attributed. Indeed, classical political economy was itself an amazing hybrid, part science and part sheer superstition. As a science, it dispensed altogether with divine sanctions such as medieval social preachment had invoked to sustain the doctrine of just price and condemn the growing commercialism of the age. But the laws of nature—with which, after the fashion of the age of reason, it re-

placed the laws of God—virtually deified commercialism. As Lewis Mumford once wrote, in the clearest and most succinct characterization of our traditional economic ideology that I have ever seen:

In the nineteenth century, capitalistic industry sought to work on the assumption that economic life was self-equilibrating. Human needs would be satisfied, and human purposes served, if each economic agent worked with no thought for anything but his immediate gain: the largest possible profit in the shortest time. Behind this theory was a sublime and now incredible theology: the conception that order is so far preordained in human affairs that a multitude of blind actions and reactions will bring it to pass. This theology was a superstition.[1]

That academic economics—the formulation and elaboration of the theory Mr. Mumford has so neatly characterized—has affected the course of modern history, seems to me unquestionable. But it is important not to exaggerate, and especially not to misconceive, the nature of this influence. Unquestionably the lay community has been confirmed in its confidence that all things work together for good to them that love money, by the solid and reassuring fact of the existence of an immense mass of highly recondite analysis presumed by its many authors to establish the truth of the popular belief. But the belief did not have its origin in that recondite analysis. On the contrary, the analysis had its origin in the antecedent and underlying belief, just as did the theology of the medieval scholastics.

The decisive fact was the dualism itself; and this dualism arose at the very dawn of modern times, long before the elaborate formulas of the political economists. For some such reasons as those I have indicated, that dualism followed an ancient pattern. Veblen, who gave more thought to this problem than any other economist has done, making it virtually the pivot of his whole analysis, at one time emphasized the "interstices" of industrial organization as the points at which financial considerations prevail over industrial ones. Within a given industrial enterprise, he thought, considerations of industrial (technological) efficiency prevailed; whereas financial

---

[1] From the Foreword to *Planned Society: Yesterday, Today, Tomorrow*, edited by Findlay MacKenzie (New York: Prentice-Hall, 1937), p. v.

considerations were paramount in the larger business strategy by which one firm sought to get the better of others, and so of the community generally. As a matter of strategy, this may be correct. But as a matter of thinking—and, as no one knew better than Veblen, such a dualism is a matter of inveterate mental habit— the disposition to envisage the facts of economic life in financial (or, as Veblen usually said, pecuniary) terms covered the entire field of economic activity.

It began by the identification of wealth with money. As everybody knows, the word "wealth" has the same root source as the word "well," an identification which still persists in the word "commonwealth" or "commonweal." To modern students of economics, accustomed as they are to subtler expressions, this crude substitution has always been extremely puzzling, especially in view of the early identification of money with gold bullion. It now seems impossible that anybody sufficiently thoughtful to have become the author of an economic tract could have fallen victim to such an egregious error as the confusion of "real wealth" with bullion; and this confusion is further compounded by the repudiation of such mercantilist follies by Adam Smith and his successors.

But students of the twenty-first century may be equally puzzled by our own obtuseness; for it will be evident to them that the followers of Adam Smith have been victims of the same confusion. To be sure, they have substituted an intangible "unit of pecuniary measurement," as they call it, for the crude bullionism of earlier days, just as later metaphysicians replaced the crude anthropomorphism of simple faith with the ineffability of the "absolute." But the effect, in both cases, has been to heighten the effect of the dualism— in one case, that of thought and things, and, in the other, that of finance and industry.

Only in the twentieth century is this dualism beginning to give way. That, I think, is the significance of our present general concern with full production. After several centuries of unbroken preoccupation with pecuniary considerations, we are beginning to think in terms of "industrial potential."

We owe this momentous change to a combination of circumstances. Most important, I think, is our growing and now decisive
awareness of industrial technology, and of its continuity with
science. Many circumstances have contributed to this development,
so many, perhaps, as to make any attempt to identify particular ones
unnecessary and even futile. Perhaps it is enough to realize that the
gradual but cumulative and accelerating growth of the natural
sciences and the industrial arts, and of all the instruments, tools,
materials, and appurtenances of every kind that go with them, has
made it inevitable that the community should eventually come to
appreciate the momentousness of this development and the significance of the whole aspect of community life in which it has occurred. Nevertheless certain incidents do stand out as typical and
suggestive of the character of the whole development.

One such is the appearance of the automobile. This seems to me
important because the automobile is by far the most complicated
piece of apparatus that has ever come into use as a feature of
virtually every household in the land. Another is the transplanta-
tion of the chemical industry. This began with the severance of
German chemical imports in 1914 and the subsequent confiscation
of German patents, together with the chemical requirements of
war. Neither of these incidents is qualitatively unique. Thus, for
example, the radio has brought electrical sophistication to the whole
community, much as the automobile brought mechanical sophistication. Furthermore, the educational influence of the automobile
is not qualitatively different from that of farm machinery. Indeed,
that is what makes the automobile significant, just as the qualitative
continuity of chemical with other industry is what makes that industry significant. Before 1914 it used to be said that Americans
lacked the chemical "faculty." American "genius" was for mechanical apparatus only. So also it used to be said that this "genius" was
confined to a few mechanically "gifted" individuals; that "ordinary"
persons could never expect to understand what makes an engine
go; and that no woman would ever be capable of driving such a
vehicle, let alone of understanding it. All these superstitions have

been eroded away in a single generation, and by just such developments as these.

To this cumulative series of technological incidents the great depression of the nineteen-thirties added another incident of quite a different type. This is true not because the depression was a calamity, but because it revealed more clearly than ever before certain aspects of the economy which our industrial maturity was already bringing into focus. During the depression a community which had already begun to learn to think in terms of machines received a clear demonstration of the connection between machines and general prosperity. Rolling mills stopped rolling and turret lathes stopped turning because people failed to buy their output; people failed to buy because they were unemployed; they were unemployed because the machines had stopped.

I shall not discuss the paradox of want in the midst of plenty. Orthodox economists still protest that the word "abundance," which came into such general use during these years, is both meaningless and misleading. But orthodoxy no longer enjoys a clear field. One of the major consequences of the depression, as everybody knows, was the rapid spread of new ways of thinking among professional economists. These ideas were, of course, not altogether new, and they were not precipitated out of historical events, so to speak, untouched by human hand. But events affect the focus of attention of academic minds no less than those of the whole community. It is beyond question, I think, that the problems and even the procedures with which so many economists are preoccupied today have been to a very considerable extent forced upon their attention by actual events; and that the work of pioneers in the new ways of thinking —most particularly, of course, J. M. Keynes—has been so widely and so closely studied very largely because of its obvious relevance to actual conditions.

The modern community does not receive its thoughts by hypnotic suggestion from the pundits, Trilby-fashion. Orthodoxy notwithstanding, ordinary Americans were convinced by the evidence of their own senses that the condition from which their sufferings

arose during the depression was of quite a different character from the famines by which, for example, the Oriental peoples have been cursed. I do not mean to suggest that academic thinking is socially ineffective. It is of decisive importance in the field of strategy—a point to which I shall revert shortly. Moreover, it is an essential ingredient in the process by which community convictions are precipitated out of general confusion. The scholar is a social catalyst. In a world in which the evidence of the senses is frequently at complete variance to immemorial belief, it makes a tremendous difference even to the many who do not—and perhaps cannot—read professional literature to know that professional students also see and seriously consider what appears even to the eyes of the untutored as a plain and obvious fact. In its time, classical political economy performed this function. Certainly it credited the fact, and the importance, of economic development, thereby confirming common experience in the face of immemorial tradition which held the whole economic life process to be unworthy of serious consideration. To be sure, it also confirmed the community in a pestilential dualism. But it did so under circumstances which, perhaps, made that inevitable; and with a change of circumstances, professional students are now confirming the community in its new realism.

Among the incidents which have combined to such effect, the recent war also demands recognition. Whereas the depression—coming at a time when the cumulative advances of science and technology had produced a general but diffuse realization of the significance of this factor in our economic life—brought this sense to focus on the material facts of curtailed production and curtailed employment, the war afforded the most dramatic demonstration in all history of the significance of what is now generally known as "industrial potential."

Throughout this discussion I have emphasized "full production." "Industrial potential" is not quite an exact synonym, but the social significance of the two phrases is the same. "Full production" is significant precisely because it conceives "prosperity" not in pecuniary terms, but as the physical consequence of the full use of the "industrial potential." "Industrial potential" is significant because it sets up as the limiting factor of economic well-being not "solvency," or any other pecuniary concept, but the physical apparatus of industry. As the war demonstrated, it is not dollars that matter; it is thousands of tons of steel and aluminum. The London *Economist* once remarked editorially that the recent war has demonstrated once and for all that finance is not the limiting factor in any economic effort. Anything that can be done industrially—that is, within the limits of "industrial potential"—can be financed.

Such being the case, we are now well on the way to the integration of Western society—appearances to the contrary notwithstanding. What we are approaching is an integration that is based on realism, and a realism that is based on a realistic humanism. There are still those who insist that Western society has yet to determine what it wants, and even that it cannot do so by such efforts as it is now making. But has any society ever wanted the reverse of "full production"? Is our problem one of "deciding" what we want, or one of understanding what it is that we have always wanted and always struggled to achieve? To me the latter seems to be the case. That, it seems to me, is the lesson we have learned from those realistic humanists who have been our greatest teachers.

The trouble with dualism is that whatever men are, and do, and want, it tells them to be, and do, and seek *something else*. That, certainly, has been the root cause of all our economic confusion. Men have always wanted to make the most of whatever talents, whatever culture, whatever "industrial potential," they have had. But instead of proceeding simply and directly to do so, they have been diverted to seeking something else: a mystic self-identification with the "Absolute," or a pot of gold at the end of an economic rainbow, conceived as the maximization of satisfactions. Since satisfactions are by definition incommensurable, nobody knows what is the maximum of satisfactions, unless it is the state of affairs that happens to prevail; and nobody knows how to achieve it, unless by letting events take their course. Strangely enough, such paths have led us to confusion!

But "industrial potential" is knowable. It is even subject to fairly precise measurement. Moreover, it is something which it is well within our powers to enlarge—as witness the tremendous enlargement of the American industrial potential during the recent war. We know what "full production" is, and everybody now recognizes it as something we all want, and have always wanted. To be sure, old habits are still strong upon us. We want nothing changed. The National Association of Manufacturers wants full production, but it also wants no interference by government in the freedom of great corporations to do as they like with their own. The Congress of Industrial Organizations wants full production, but it also wants to stop work whenever there is an advantage to be gained by doing so. Clearly, much remains to be done. But when the N.A.M. and the C.I.O. agree that we all want full production, it seems to me impossible that we shall continue to tolerate want in the midst of plenty.

12

Max Otto: A Biographical Note

G. C. SELLERY

Dean Emeritus, College of Letters and Sciences, University of Wisconsin

PROFESSOR MAX CARL OTTO, in whose honor the foregoing essays were written, was born in the historic town of Zwickau, Saxony, in 1876, and was brought to America by his immigrant parents in his fifth year. He went to school, through the sixth grade, in Wheeling, West Virginia, where his father kept a restaurant. He studied the Lutheran catechism diligently under a stern, old-fashioned pastor, and also learned to concentrate so thoroughly on what he heard in church that he could repeat the essentials of the sermon to his Lutheran parents. The resulting development of the power of concentration has stood him in good stead ever since.

Young Max served as a waiter in the family restaurant until he was sixteen. Then he went off to Cincinnati and Chicago on his own. In Chicago he was employed as a messenger for the R. G. Dun rating agency, and did incidental human salvage work on Sundays for the Y.M.C.A. This latter avocation led to a regular quasi-religious post in the Milwaukee Y.M.C.A., where he worked with boys. But, recognizing the need for further education if he was to "grasp this sorry scheme of things," he gave up his job in the Y.M.C.A. and filled in some of the many gaping holes in his preparation for college by study in local academies. This accomplished, he was admitted, somewhat irregularly, to Carroll College, Wauke-sha, by President Rankin, who was not averse to stretching the rules in favor of a young man of obvious ability and persistence. From Carroll, after a couple of fruitful years, he passed on to the state university at Madison, where he majored in history under the great Frederick Jackson Turner, and secured a distinguished B.A. in 1906, with election to Phi Beta Kappa. (At Wisconsin also the rules were stretched—or rather broken—in his favor, for he, whose prose is so simple and strong, had not taken the required course in freshman English.)

After admission to the bachelor's degree, Mr. Otto took up graduate studies in philosophy under the guidance of Professors McGilvary and Sharp, and won his Ph.D. in 1911. The tutorship or direction of the studies of another young American enabled Mr. Otto to spend a summer and a semester in Europe, with a term under Windelband at Heidelberg. He had been appointed assistant in philosophy at Wisconsin in 1908 and instructor in 1910, and there he rubbed shoulders and sharpened wits with Boyd H. Bode and Horace M. Kallen, and other promising fledglings in philosophy, while beginning his ascent of the academic ladder to a full professorship in 1921. A year earlier he was married to Rhoda Owen, a graduate of Wisconsin and a history teacher; and later on he spent with her seven productive months of travel and study in Europe. They have a son and a daughter.

Mr. Otto has also produced, under his wife's critical eye, three good books with significant titles: *Things and Ideals* (1924), *Natural Laws and Human Hopes* (1926) and *The Human Enterprise* (1940), together with a large sheaf of periodical articles, public lectures, reviews, and contributions to other critical volumes. His share in the controversial *Is There a God?* (1932), originally a running debate in *The Christian Century,* with H. N. Wieman and D. C. Macintosh as his antagonists, reveals with clarity the antitheistic position he has reached, as does his chapter in *Religious Liberals Reply* (1947). His address in the centenary volume, *William James: The Man and The Thinker* (1942), naturally discloses much of his own philosophical position, which is briefly but cogently set forth in his chapters in *Philosophy in American Edu-*

cation (1945), a report by Brand Blanshard and four other members of the commission appointed by the American Philosophical Association to investigate the subject. Here Mr. Otto makes clear his conception of the important role which "functional philosophy" may be made to play in the education of American college youth.

Mr. Otto's service as a teacher of philosophy, and as chairman of the department of philosophy at Wisconsin since 1936, came to an end in 1947, when he became a professor emeritus. He has taught in summer sessions across the country, from Harvard and Minnesota to U.C.L.A., has declined much more lucrative posts elsewhere in favor of stormy but stimulating Wisconsin, has been honored with the presidency of the Western branch of the American Philosophical Association, and is still productively busy with articles, reviews, and public lectures on important occasions.

The philosophy which Max Otto has at heart is not any of the abstract, deductive systems which ingenious minds have invented through the ages to explain the universe and man in whole or in part; it is not the sort of philosophy one finds in the older histories of the subject. Of course he knows these systems, and he has been heard to say that he would give his right arm—"well, at least a little finger"—to read the lost treatise of Protagoras on *Truth,* for its possible anticipation of pragmatism, of which he himself is a representative. Pragmatism is in fact essentially an American product, native, democratic, homespun, redolent of the soil. It grows out of and is rooted in the common problems and common sense of men and women—refined common sense, of course, but still common sense, whether at work in business, agriculture, politics, economics, science, or religion. The underlying purpose of this philosophy is the enhancement of human life for all. "Humane, warm, and in the best sense simple," President Burkhardt of Bennington has well said of Max Otto, "his wisdom is pervaded by a profound sense of dedication to the enrichment of man's intellectual and spiritual life."

Max Otto's philosophy was conceived in Wisconsin, the state which had quickly wrapped its tendrils around his heart. He himself has made that clear in many ways, in none more explicitly than in his address before the Wisconsin branch of the American Association of University Professors, which was promptly published *in extenso* in *The Capital Times* of April 6, 1947. Here, after characterizing the great teachers of his student days at Wisconsin, he said:

In a word, my professors were centers of aggressive intellectual energy, sources of cultural vision. They were not teachers of lessons; their classes were outposts in the recurring struggle between enlightenment and superstition, between knowledge and ignorance. And their students were apprentices in the same high adventure. In and through and around these informing, mind-stretching class-room exercises vibrated . . . the active educational philosophy of President Van Hise, expanding, enriching, deepening the influence that was at work upon our minds and hearts.

And then he quoted from Van Hise's commencement address of 1912—to be discussed on a later page—and from his N.E.A. address of July 4, 1916, where he sweepingly declares:

A university must insist that the whole domain of physical and human phenomena belongs with[in] its scope—pure science, applied science, politics, morals, religion, are proper fields of study for a university. No part of the domain of human experience, knowledge or ideas can be set off as forbidden ground.

Yes, Max Otto's philosophy was conceived—and born—in Wisconsin. Of course his native endowment of mind and heart, his experiences of life, and his struggles for clarity of purpose underlie the vision he caught at the university. One may also safely assert that the elder La Follette's program for social betterment had a part in Max Otto's philosophy, and that it was nurtured, enriched, and confirmed by the teachings of William James and of John Dewey —especially of John Dewey, his good and great friend.

Dickinson S. Miller, a surviving comrade of William James, in a letter he sent to the writer of this note a few years ago, delineates briefly but fully the characteristic functionalism or instrumentalism of Max Otto's philosophy.

Philosophy has, in my belief, two distinct justifications. It has a right to be pursued for its own sake, as a worthy subject of thought, a high form of consciousness, an end and not a means. But it also may be pursued as an aid to humanity, as lighting up our way before us, as a potent means for the uplifting of life. And of these two the latter is overwhelmingly more important and urgent. Philosophy has in the latter respect decisive things to give.

Max Otto has meant much to me on both sides. On both sides I have learned from him. A test is this. I find myself rereading articles and looking anew into books of his and thinking again of remarks he has made. I must say this, and I say it deliberately: more, far more, than any other philosopher I have known at any time he has stood for the second and more momentous status of the study. In purpose and in vigorous realistic thought he has made philosophy serve humanity. His heart and head are at one. In considering American philosophy at large today, its character is raised for me when I think of Otto.

Within the broad reaches of his philosophy, Max Otto, a man of genuine religious temper, places stress on the need of our age for a nontheistic faith. The writer ventures to quote from his own review of *The Human Enterprise,* written when that important book was published:

The theistic foundation of truth, goodness, beauty, and humane feeling being seriously weakened [Mr. Otto argues], it is an urgent requirement of the times that an alternative foundation be found for those who do not accept the theistic foundation. This other foundation the author finds in practical sympathy for the needs of mankind as they progressively reveal themselves in the working out of the actual problems which confront humanity.

Max Otto's abandonment of supernaturalism, which he pushed to its extreme limits in the debate with Wieman and Macintosh mentioned above, involved him in serious difficulties almost from the beginning of his career as a teacher at Wisconsin. For it inevitably colored what became his great and increasingly popular course, "Man and Nature," where he takes a frankly naturalistic view of the universe. The first attack came in 1912, when clerical critics and their sympathizers in Madison and elsewhere in the state demanded his elimination from the staff as an enemy of religion, and, strangely enough, as a violator of the state constitution, which forbids sectarian religious instruction in the university. The stamina of the young instructor was put to a very tough test. It would have been an easy way out to give up the course; but Max Otto, after prolonged reflection, declined to do so. His students and not a few of his colleagues—some of whom hardly knew him—stood by him, and Van Hise, the great president, irritated though he was by this additional disturbance, in effect backed him up in his forthright commencement address of that year (1912), entitled "The Spirit of a University."

Freedom of thought, Van Hise here declared, inquiry after truth for its own sake, adjustment of the knowledge of the past in the light of the newest facts and highest reason—"this is the essential spirit of a university, *which under no circumstances should it yield.*"

Whether the subject taught be that of the language or history of a people, knowledge of the universe without reference to the wants of man, or the applications of this knowledge to his needs, is a matter of indifference; provided only this broad, inexorable, noncompromising spirit . . . to follow wherever truth may lead . . . be maintained.

This spirit, President Van Hise proclaims, "forever makes a university a center of conflict. If a university were content to teach simply those things concerning which there is practical unanimity of opinion . . . there would be quiet; but it would be the quiet of stagnation." (One cannot but think of Max Otto's belief in the great educative value of "controversial subjects.")

Van Hise's defense of *Lehrfreiheit* included the tactful admonition that

. . . the university is no place for either the agitator or the pedant. . . . Different views should be fully and fairly presented in order that the student may be aware of all the essential facts bearing in every direction and thus be fully able to appreciate the different points of view. Having pursued this method, a professor . . . has the right to express his personal views and convictions, provided it be done with humility and with the realization that ultimate truth has nowhere been reached, that the advance of tomorrow may modify the statement of today.

Mr. Otto's teaching—he himself is not mentioned or referred to—never received a more satisfying defense.

It is of interest to note that in the revision of this 1912 commencement address, which he read on May 23, 1913, to the Philadelphia City Club's expedition to the university, President Van Hise explicitly included religion (along with sociology, morals, and politics) as a proper subject for university investigation—"with the certainty," to be sure, "that it will never reach perfection anywhere, at any time, with regard to anything."

Max Otto's student following and influence grew steadily in the following decades, and many liberal theologians gave him their enduring friendship. Nevertheless, he was exposed to three more bitter attacks. In the latest and fiercest of these, that of 1932, he, a professor in politics, was used as a whipping boy for his friends, the LaFollettes, and was assailed in press and platform as an exhibit of the pernicious radicalism—and atheism—they were said to foster. But again students and colleagues, in increasing numbers, rallied to his side, and again the president of the university, now Glenn Frank, defended him—as his predecessors had done in each of the preceding attacks—and his opponents were thereafter reduced to occasional and ineffective sniping. Max Otto had won—the university had won—a veritable "Twenty Years' War." His steadfastness and serenity during these years of tension were equally remarkable. Nevertheless, one may be permitted to conjecture that he has had more than enough of one "controversial subject."

Professor Otto's knowledge of scientific method and scientific achievements is wide and deep. It is conveniently shown in a pocket-size book entitled *Science and the Moral Life* (1949), which consists of selections from his writings. (It is one of the series called "Mentor Books," published by the New American Library.) Mr. Otto is not blind to some of the perilous fruits of science, notably the atomic bomb, and he does not exculpate their propagators. But scientific method, he is certain, must be extended to the social and of course to the religious field, to what he calls the search for the good life. Scientific method, he makes clear, is a way of investigation which relies solely on disciplined empirical observation and rigorously exact proof, proof that extends beyond inner or personal conviction to outer or public demonstration:

The significance of objectivity sought in terms of method instead of subject matter is obviously far-reaching. Its relevancy to the problem of a socially responsive and a socially responsible science need not be pointed out.

The objectively testable kind of thinking which is the rule in the natural sciences should be put to work in the great laboratory of man's search for the good life—the good life richly and profoundly conceived.[1]

The search for the good life, to Max Otto, involves not only economic reconstruction in the interest of the fairest distribution of earth's bounties to all men, but also political action to promote this distribution. "Unless enough Americans," he declared in 1939, "are willing to invest their idealism in the project of remaking our social order into a positive means for utilizing our resources for the common good, it will not be long before there will be no idealism to invest."[2]

A significant illustration of Mr. Otto's "realistic idealism," expounded in *The Human Enterprise,* is his championship of what he terms "creative bargaining." Its distinguishing marks, he says, are; "(1) An honest attempt to appreciate as fully as possible the conflicting aims as they appear to the protagonists. (2) The intuition of a new aim through which the underlying purposes at issue can be achieved, although a specific form of those purposes is surrendered. (3) The embodiment of the new aim in a practical program." This, he points out, is profoundly different from compromise, for activity here centers, not upon "splitting the difference," but upon discovering a new end which, when discovered, will profit all who are involved.[3]

In an article, "War and Moral Progress," published in *The Progressive* for September, 1949, Mr. Otto, after observing that the

---

[1] Pages 96–97, 122.
[2] Page 192.
[3] *Science and the Moral Life,* p. 67.

task of social redemption cannot be accomplished by detachment from practical affairs, again presses for the employment of creative bargaining,

. . . a getting together to wrestle with a controversy in order that it may be made to yield the amplest good for all who have a stake in the outcome, including an interested segment of "the public.". . . Let the adherents of political and economic groups, of educational, aesthetic, and religious projects, sharpen their sense of what they stand for; let them envisage and appreciate the purposes of those who are opposed; let them cooperate in originating and perfecting methods of arriving at agreed-upon next steps toward the general welfare—and they will be taking part in the furtherance of moral progress.

And he ends his article with a declaration of faith:

Faith in the human cause is not rooted in thinking, but it does not ripen into fruit without thinking. And the art we need to learn more than any other is how by joint, cooperative thinking we may gather the fruits of peace under conditions of animosity and strife.

Max Otto is a man of many talents. His intimacy with his students in lecture, conference, office, and home is exceptional. His friendly converse with people is not restricted to academic folk, young and old: wherever he travels, on train or road, or in the open spaces he loves, he is likely to talk with the men and women and children he meets up with and these casual contacts help to explain his confidence in the fundamental good sense of the plain people. Indeed it does not seem extravagant to think that they have had something to do with his philosophy, with his belief in the "potentialities of human nature." He loves the earthly scene and stands reverent before the mysteries of the universe and of life. He finds further solace in great music and good literature. His skill with the pencil is worthy of a great illustrator. His dialectical competence makes him a formidable antagonist, and his wit and humor render his company a delight to his many friends.

One of his teachers at Carroll College, Mr. E. G. Ehlman, a life-long intimate, not long ago painted this word picture of him:

I was teaching at Carroll College when Mr. Otto enrolled, and we soon became warm friends. In my teaching experience of forty years I have met many men of great ability and sterling character; but for all around ability, versatility, integrity, wit and humor, ingenuity, sympathetic understanding, courage, refinement, and the finer qualities of heart and mind, I know of no one who excels him.

One of his journalistic opponents in the 1932 attack praised him in his newspaper as a fine gentleman, an honest home man, a man who loves nature and children, an unassuming individual who is neither sinister nor cynical. "He is a lovable character, his is a winning personality"—*but* . . .

These tributes, satisfying indeed so far as they go—and they go far—lack illustrative detail.

Quite the most comprehensive view of Max Otto was exhibited —as in a multiple mirror—at Madison on May 6, 1947, at a banquet celebrating his academic career. It was presented by a graduate student and a group of men who know him intimately. Their testimony, stenographically recorded with other incidental remarks, was published in Madison, later in the year, as *The Max C. Otto Jubilee Addresses*. From this brochure the writer of this note borrows their tributes. It is his belief that the quoted words carry not only convincing detail but also something of the atmosphere which enveloped the speakers, the special guests, and the six hundred students, former students, and other friends of the Ottos who listened to the memorable addresses.

The dinner program, which was conducted by the writer of this note, was opened by him with a brief introduction, which ended with these words:

Those are the characteristics of the great teacher: mastery of his subject; ability to communicate it and evoke an appreciation of exact knowledge and clear thinking; and ability to convey it by means of his personality. One or two great teachers are enough to lift a college faculty, through example and beneficent contagion, to a position of distinction. Three or four such teachers are all that one can expect to find in a great university. I have been at Wisconsin since 1901. Figure it out. I have been here since 1901, and in my forty years and more I think it safe to declare that we have had eleven great teachers, beginning with my beloved master and friend, Frederick Jackson Turner, and ending with Max Otto. These teachers have helped the rest of us to amount to something. The one I begin with is Turner; the one I end with is Otto. No one of the eleven is greater than Otto.

Then came, *inter alia,* the addresses (the gracious opening sentences are omitted). Mrs. Joyce Erdman, a graduate student at Wisconsin, led off:

As an apprentice [speaker] this evening, I am supposed to tell a story. It runs somewhat like a fairy tale. Once upon a time at this university there was an engineer, a senior, who felt that, after three and a half years of study, of grinding and poring over books, he was entitled to a bit of leisure in his last semester. He combed through the college catalogue and finally noticed a philosophy course—"Types of Humanism." This engineer did not know what the title meant, but he felt fairly safe, because he had heard that philosophy was just a lot of talk and thought modestly to himself that he was good at "shooting the bull," so he entered the course. Here is the magic to the fairy tale. That boy was transformed from a student whose world was bound by lathes and blue prints to a questioning thinker within the period of that fifteen-week course. He found that he did not want to sleep through the class because it was too interesting; he was afraid he would miss some of the things he wanted to hear. Never before, in four years of college, had he been stimulated to evaluate his life's standards. Never before had ideas become so vitally alive to him. His was more or less the old story. He had passively accepted what had been handed to him—his religious beliefs, social conventions, and attitudes toward his fellow-beings. Now he stripped the wrappings from these ready-packaged attitudes and he examined them under a new light—a broad and natural sunlight of human relations. Then, outside the classroom, he found that his own world seemed actually different. He found a variety of new experiences were open to him. He began to do some unheard-of things. He began to attend our well-known university convocation lectures. He wanted to find out what was going on. He made friends with students with totally different backgrounds. He went to the various churches to discover what people believed, and why. All the time he was trying to relate his new ideas to actual experience. At the beginning I alluded to this as a fairy tale. And it has a certain magic in it—that magical transformation. Yet it is not a fairy tale. It is a true story. I know the boy. I have seen the change.

I would like to emphasize that that experience is not a unique one, for that engineer's experience has happened to every student, in one degree or another, in Professor Otto's classes. That, to me and to all of you, is a very wonderful accomplishment, for students get something out of these classes which is rarely received in a university education. Professor Otto gives us an initiation into maturity. More specifically, he shows us the possibilities within our own lives. From him we gain a sense of direction, and yet it is never a single direction or a single system, for there is never indoctrination in Professor Otto's classes. I would much rather be sitting down here now, listening to Professor Otto talk, as you all would. Then we would all understand why Professor Otto's lectures are so warm and real. He has a remarkable method of presentation. He completely forgets that traditional student-professor attitude— the professor on the rostrum speaking down to us, the uninformed. Professor Otto talks to us as individuals, who are not so much seeking knowledge of the transcendental world as trying to discover intelligent, down-to-earth, practical methods with which to approach and guide everyday conduct. All of you who at one time or another were in Professor Otto's classes, or are in them now, or have just talked to him for hours on end—you all know his very casual conversational talks. They are full of quiet ideas of what man can make of man—of scientific methods—of the miracle and greatness of nature. Yet, throughout, they are always sprinkled with a humor that genuinely makes us laugh to ourselves at a mixed-up world.

I am afraid a lot of what I have been saying sounds something like so many platitudes. It is not meant to sound that way. Yet I do find it difficult to express to Professor Otto the students' gratitude for the ideas that he has put before us. Recently I asked many students just what meant the most to them in Professor Otto's classes. First of all, they prefaced their answers with something like this: "What a guy! That man is really all right." Then they went on to say that Professor Otto had given them something to think about. He had made them critically analyze and question their own lives. Where were they going? What did they believe? What were they going to do with their lives? So, for the moment, if we just put aside his other great attributes—his wonderful humor, his genuine interest in students, his forward and very progressive vision—Professor Otto has achieved a very wonderful goal. He has extended his "militant interest in man's earthly enterprise" to his students. He has made them think and aspire to the greatness he exemplifies. So, for that, we thank Professor Otto, and we join in celebrating his great achievement at this university.

Frederick Burkhardt, then of the department of philosophy at Wisconsin, now president of Bennington College, followed:

I see my function as that of telling you a few of the things I have come to learn about Max Otto as a colleague of his—as a student of his, too, for a time—and to tell you what I think has made him a great teacher and a great educator. I subscribe, of course, to the definition that Mr. Sellery gave you of what a great teacher is, but I do not want to refer to those aspects of Mr. Otto. I want to talk about a few other aspects that have struck me rather personally, and I shall try to be as brief as possible about it.

I have to start with a story, though. I heard it just the other day. It is about a well-known professor of English literature at one of the Scottish universities, who had been teaching the same course in English literature for over forty years. It seems that as he looked up from his notes in one lecture, he saw a student with his arms crossed, taking no notes. He became irritated about it and said, "Why are you not taking any notes?" The student said, "I have my father's."

I submit that that is the kind of story no one will ever hear about Max Otto. The reason one will not hear it takes some explaining, I think. The reason Max has never been able to give the same lecture twice is that he has learned so much in the interim. He is a great teacher because he has never stopped learning. In my eleven years of knowing him he has never stopped learning. That, to me, is his great characteristic as an educator—his freshness and openness of mind. That freshness and openness of mind make him today the youngest man in our department.

Another reason is that there are some professors—happily not many, I think—who lecture and teach as though they were having a dialogue with God. There are others who write their lectures as though they were talking to their colleagues in the same field. Max Otto is not like that. He makes his lectures for students. He does not mind if God and the professors are listening, but he composes them for students.

I think every man and woman here who has been a student of Max Otto is aware of how conscious he is of his audience, of the people whom he is talking to. He has been known in classes of hundreds of people to notice the absence of this one, that one, or the other one. He is constantly commenting to the students at the end of his lecture on how they responded. He is aware of them as individual people. He is thinking of them in that way. I think there is definite proof of how constantly aware he is of the students, because if you have ever been in his study, there is a motto on the wall, which you see as you go out of the study and start down the stairs. It is written in beautiful Gothic lettering. I suppose he sees it every morning. It says: "Don't give them two bad ones in a row."

There is another characteristic that I had quite a time understanding, because I had to be re-educated by Max Otto. That is his simplicity. It is very deceptive because it looks as though he comes by things so easily. After eleven years under his tutelage I have come to understand how extremely difficult it is to be simple. He has got the simplicity that takes tremendously hard work, and every lecture he has given is hard labor. I have heard him give lectures that reminded me of Bach's sonatas: they had purity, clarity, and simplicity—like the sonatas they required not only genius, but tremendously hard work.

There is another characteristic that strikes me time and again, and that is his active search for the controversial. I have heard him say frequently that the only really educating subjects are controversial ones. He has a nose for them. When he finds them, he does not go about glossing over the difficulties and differences. He sees his job as deepening or clarifying—straightening out what the difficulty is, rather than patching it up. Then he takes a position because he is no mere disinterested spectator. He is an active participant in these living issues. I was just thinking, as I was wondering what I should say tonight, how that sense of actively participating and getting interested is reflected in his one big vice—he is an inveterate gambler. He is the easiest man in the world to get a bet with. He will bet on the National League pennant, the weather, the date the lakes will freeze over, and the sex of your next baby. I have been betting with him for eleven years, and I think that one of the reasons he is that way is that he just does not want merely to see things develop. He wants to take sides in the development. He wants to have a stake in it, and he bets on it because it gives him a stake in it. I personally think it is a very deep aspect of the man. In eleven years of betting I regret to say he is usually right.

These are the aspects of the teacher that produce the results that Mrs. Erdman told you about. I have also known him as chairman of the department. As chairman of the department, he has reflected all of these characteristics. As chairman of the department, I think his major aim has been to get a group of individuals to form a team which would be united in the common interest, whatever their philosophical outlooks and philosophical interests as philosophers might be—united in the common vision of being interested in the philosophies of students and in seeing that they are provided with the tools, with the techniques, with the disciplines, that will enable them to fashion their own philosophies. He never has had the attitude that philosophy was something that could be dished out in neat little packages.

I have been a member of that team. I am very glad and very grateful that I have been. I can assure you that being a part of that team has given a sense of excitement—a sense of mission—and a sense of being part of an enterprise that is truly creative.

The teacher and the philosopher and the chairman are only three facets of a very complex and, I think, great human being. All of us assembled here tonight—and we are just a fraction of those who would be here if they could—all of us are tied to this man by invisible but strong cords, of one sort or another. We are all very different, diverse individuals and personalities, yet we all have these cords leading to Max. I have thought the reason for that is the greatness of his humanity, because I think we see in him some aspects of something we each would like to be. When we see it in him, we get encouragement from it. We feel it is worthwhile, and we feel it is possible of attainment. That is why, as we think of him, we feel a little stronger and a little warmer, and we feel very happy that he has come into our lives.

Samuel Rogers of the French department at Wisconsin, novelist and musician, was the next speaker:

For I don't know how many years Max Otto has kept open house for his students, colleagues, and all his friends on Saturday afternoons. It was that side of him as a host in his own house that I was asked to talk to you about tonight. I was told that others would describe him as a teacher, philosopher, etc.

My first feeling is that Max is the kind of man who can't be cut up into compartments, who can't be dissected. You have all known lecturers whose whole personality seems to change the moment they step on the platform. Their appearance is different from their ordinary appearance. Their voice is different. They may be charming in private conversation and brilliant lecturers, but you feel you are dealing with two distinct people. It is rather different, I think, with Max. He is a terribly complicated person, and yet somehow he always manages to remain himself. It makes no difference, as Mrs. Erdman suggested, whether he is talking to a large class of students in Bascom Hall or to a few friends in his house. At Bascom Hall, luckily, more people are able to hear him. But there is, after all, a kind of difference, when you think of Max in his house, because when you think of him in his home, you never think of him by himself. You always think of Max and

Rhoda together—the delightful, warm and exciting atmosphere of that house is obviously always a work of perfect cooperation. But, here again, I run into a difficulty. It seems to me that when a man talks in public or when he writes books, he must expect to be talked about. He may dislike it intensely, but there is simply no help for it. If the worst comes to the worst, he may have to attend banquets and listen to speeches in his honor. It is his hard luck. There is nothing he can do about it. But people normally have a right to be left in peace in the privacy of their own homes. I am convinced that Rhoda and Max would be embarrassed and distressed were I to give anything like a candid camera shot of them—the kind of thing you might read in a film magazine about a movie star; so I think the best way I know is simply to try to give my own impression of the house and those afternoons as quickly as I can —the afternoons so many of their friends enjoyed so many years—and to say nothing here directly about either Rhoda or Max.

In the first place, you would find there in their sitting room people of all ages and all kinds. Obviously shy and diffident students, who stammer, hesitate, and blush the way I have been doing now, when I started to speak, might be sitting on the sofa next to a distinguished philosopher. Here would be a wonderful thing. Mrs. Erdman spoke of magic. There was magic in it. Before you knew it, the student would forget he was shy, and, what was even more wonderful, the philosopher would forget he was distinguished. They would talk quite naturally as man to man. There would not be the slightest feeling of hierarchy. There was never any constraint. The only difficult or even remotely painful thing about those afternoons was trying to tear yourself away after you'd had several cups of coffee and more than your share of Rhoda's delicious coffee cake, so that the poor Otto family could get their dinner. What was the talk about? Many of you, of course, know. It was about anything under the sun. No topic was forbidden. The talk could be as serious as possible; but with Max and Rhoda there it could never be solemn, pompous, or dogmatic. It could be as frivolous as you like, but it would never be cheap or merely trifling. I think one of the remarkable things is that it could shift from the serious to the gay, and then back to the serious, in just a moment. I would say it was most characteristic—particularly when Max was talking—when it was both serious and gay at the same moment.

When I look back over those afternoons—and I am sure that many of you must look back over them too—you must feel with me that it is almost impossible to dissociate them from that particular room, with the sofa opposite the fireplace, and often a flower or two, or an arrangement of winter twigs, in a small vase on the right-hand corner of the mantlepiece—with the view, at one end, of the garden, and at the other end out through a fringe of trees to Lake Wingra. You think of them always in terms of that room. It seems to me, if you look back, beneath the surface, and beneath that special local color, you can think of those afternoons as fitting in perfectly with any number of different times and places—with any time and place where civilized people, who have loved both men and ideas, and have been quite unimpressed by dignities and titles, have invited their friends to their house to talk with them and to talk with each other.

Alain Locke of Howard University, who a year earlier had been a visiting professor of philosophy at Wisconsin, then made his contribution:

This is a philosophical tribute, and I make no apology for it, because, after all, the dull syllables have only to be thrown at the feet of our friend, while all around is the warm human love that we all feel, and that other speakers have already expressed.

When Socrates was the age of the friend whom we are honoring to-night—and perhaps that's telling on you, Max, since all students of philosophy, it can safely be assumed, remember that much—he, Socrates, said he still had an unrealized ambition: he wanted to become a musician. There's no record even in Plato as to just what the friends and disciples said, whether they kidded him on the face value of his words or paid him the deeper compliments which were his due. But someone among them could and should have said, before he himself solved the riddle, "Socrates, you know you have been making beautiful music all your life, as you, yourself of all people ought to know." For just as the truest musician is not the man who makes music, but he whose creative love of it inspires it, so the great philosophers are not the greatest theory-makers but those whose love of truth and wisdom inspires and teaches others to evoke from their own experiences insight and wisdom for the understanding of life. It is such Socratic music that Max Otto has been making all his active teaching life, and tonight's tribute, in which it is an honor and delight to share, is a human sounding board set up to catch and focus the echo, so that friends, colleagues, former and present students can more vividly hear and appreciate the pattern and harmony of such creative teaching and such consistent living. And it ought to make music even to Max Otto's ears; surely it does to ours.

It has not been easy to make, this intellectual sort of harmony, for there are all sorts of natural discords in life, not to mention the professional ones among the philosophers and the various philosophies. But for the teacher-philosopher, whose aim is self and mutual understanding, human harmony is the chief end of wisdom and the search for wisdom. Such a conception of philosophy has so characterized Max Otto that, even if he had not styled himself a humanist, those of us who have been his students, privileged curricular ones like most of you, extra-curricular ones like all the rest of us, would have called him a humanist, and a great one at that. For to all who have experienced his teaching and benefited from it, there has been much more to it than the statement of a philosophical creed or position. Almost without exception there has been the adventure of a living, human experience, an inspiring and humane and integrating exposure to philosophy as a way of life.

Though to us, of course, he thus has become a cherished symbol of what humanism means and can mean, none of us, I am sure, would willingly violate Max Otto's modesty by overstating the connection. Humanism, he himself would be the first to remind us, is an ancient and honorable philosophical tradition which he has tried merely to re-state, extend, and justify. Nevertheless, it can truthfully be said that Max Otto has made a creative contribution to contemporary humanism by construing it more progressively and developing it more democratically. Humanism began in antiquity as the brash but necessary assertion of "man as the measure of all things." In the Renaissance this ancient view became more sensibly and objectively grounded in a more empirical doctrine of man as the "measurer of all things." Current scientific humanism, it seems to me, even more modestly and constructively proclaims man as the progressive tester of all values and as the responsible co-ordinator of all things. Construing this sovereignty of man in the world neither too individualistically nor too vaingloriously, the goal of today's humanism becomes the task of discovering in and through experience common denominators that can bring life and people into some sort of progressive harmony with their environment, with themselves, and with one another.

To humanism, so conceived, Max Otto has made, and continues to make, important constructive contributions, all of them inspired by the forward-looking outlooks of science and democracy. He urges that with due respect for individual differences, we work toward an ever-expanding harmony of common agreement, uncoerced and flexible. He rightly insists that only by tolerating others can we come fully and sanely to understand ourselves. He maintains that in morals and politics as in science only the pursuit of commonly accepted truths can reveal values broad and basic enough to warrant the name of truth. And most important of all, he points to goals of social as well as of self-understanding, through which alone a more enlightened humanity can come to be the proper measure of all things.

Meanwhile, as the humane relativist, he cautions us not to be too certain that our particular notions of what is right are wholly or finally right, and especially not to be too cocksure that someone else's partly right is wholly wrong. As a progressive pragmatist, he counsels that our separate views of truth should not divide us to the point of diverting us from the search for more objective and more widely accepted truths. As a reverent agnostic he has always challenged us to discover the uniting common denominators of our beliefs. And then chiding us in his own kindly words as "scientifically adolescent mankind," he has warned us not to despair about the future progress of humanity, since, to quote him again, "not until men in large numbers have freer access to the best fruits of civilization can we presume to say what they are capable of." And so, in this illuminating dramatization of the "human enterprise," Max Otto has presented to us a humanism to which a democratic social imagination has given a distinctive American dimension and to which a pragmatic but idealistic faith has furnished a modern scientific dynamic. Posterity will, therefore, know Max Otto not merely as a humanist but as a creative enlarger of contemporary humanistic thought.

But to offer men, collectively or singly, more truth than they have previously possessed has never been an easy task or a safe and tranquil calling. Friends of Max Otto know and appreciate the Socratic risks he has always taken, the Socratic sacrifices he has had to make, the Socratic misunderstandings he has had to experience and smilingly endure. Neither they nor he would have had it otherwise. For both know that real humanists, true lovers of mankind, have always chosen not to humor or coddle humanity in its frailties, its irrationalities, its prejudices and superstitions. Accordingly, they have always chosen to be the searching, ironic critics, the bothersome gadflies, the caustic chastisers, the provocative but challenging friends. But surely tonight in one such instance the risks, the sacrifices, and even the misunderstandings seem properly balanced and compensated. Instead of a public prosecution and a bitter cup of hemlock a more enlightened community breaks the historic precedent and offers to its oldest and best philosopher laurels of praise and a loving cup of gratitude, respect, love, and friendship.

Lloyd K. Garrison of New York, formerly for a dozen years dean of the law school at Wisconsin, was the final witness:

Max Otto schooled himself to translate into common or garden words the deepest meanings and the subtlest beauties, to state their inner essences so simply and directly that all could understand; and in talking about him I must attempt no less if I am to be true to his spirit. I never knew a philosopher less given to rhetoric and mysteries than he. He is blood brother to Socrates, who was so devoid of airs and pretended to so little knowledge that people used to go to him to be introduced to philosophers, and he would take and introduce them.

As Socrates was the child of his age, so Max is bone of Wisconsin's bone, flesh of its flesh. From its tradition, its landscape, its flora, its fauna, and its people he has drawn sustenance, and this sustenance he has impressed with his own spirit and has returned it in transmuted form to Wisconsin's sons and daughters.

What nourishment can one draw from the great Wisconsin scene? To me the chief glory of Wisconsin lies in the fact that there have been exemplified here over the course of three generations, more vividly than elsewhere, certain political and moral truths, namely, that men and institutions must either move forward or retrogress; that they move forward most freely and creatively when their aims are bold, brave, and generous; that aims of that sort cannot be achieved altogether in peace and quiet, but call for men and women with clear heads and strong nerves, who are prepared to go out into the marketplace and do battle with the forces of ignorance, bigotry, and greed; that this battle, which is really a campaign that will never quite be finished, cannot successfully be carried on by individual sorties, but requires a joining of hands and a common effort; and that this effort to make the most headway cannot be political only or intellectual only but must be a fusion of the two, with all the resources of book-learning and of university research, and the imagination and perspective of trained minds being given freely to the service of social ends through community action.

These principles form part, at least, of what used to be called the Wisconsin Idea. I say "used to be called" because it is not the fashion nowadays, as it was when I first came to Wisconsin, to talk about this idea, and I have even heard it said by people who either do not know or do not understand Wisconsin that the idea itself is moribund. I, for one, do not believe that; I believe that the idea has immense vitality; that its roots lie deep in the Wisconsin soil, and that, with only a little cultivation, it will send forth new shoots and bear new fruits as promising as any in the past.

The Wisconsin Idea has lent color and wings to Max's teaching—so much so that in his classes you can see the walls of the room dissolve and hear the tramp of humanity as it comes marching in.

But Max's teaching has a magic all its own, which cannot be described only by reference to the Wisconsin Idea. His relationship with his students is a very special one—the exact opposite of the cow and the milkmaid between whom, as Santayana said, periodic contributions pass, but there is no conversation. Even Max's lectures are like a running fire of conversation, and he has the great gift of evocation, of drawing out from his students—as from his friends—insights and formulations which they never knew were there till Max released them by his eagerness to move forward to new heights. Like the Queen in *Alice in Wonderland,* who remembered best the things that happened week after next, Max seems to stand ever in the future and to be beckoning you towards him from a secret vantage-point.

And then in his teaching, as I have heard it on a few memorable occasions—not nearly so many as I would have wished, but experience is as to intensity and not as to duration—he gives you the extraordinary sense of the totality of the human enterprise on earth, of us here on this little globe, so far as we know the only thinking things in all the vastness of time and space, produced in the course of a million million years out of the depths of sea and slime and jungle by we know not what miracles of cosmic energy; alone here for a moment between birth and death— a spectacle at once so pitiful, so tragic, and so grand that, if we could only hold it forever before our eyes, we might drop our pettinesses and our cruelties, and listen for once to the dictates of our hearts.

A great modern physicist wrote a few lines which I would like to read to you because they seem to me to be talking about Max. He said: "As inhabitants of the earth, we are living at the very beginning of time. We have come into being in the fresh glory of the dawn, and a day of almost unthinkable length stretches before us with unimaginable opportunities for accomplishment. Our descendants of far-off ages, looking down this long vista of Time from the other end, will see our present age as the misty morning of the world's history; our contemporaries of today will appear as dim heroic figures who fought their way through jungles of ignorance, error, and superstition to discover truth, to learn how to harness the forces of nature, and to make a world worthy for mankind to live in."

In the ranks of these heroic figures stands the friend whom we have met tonight to honor. He has given us a new faith in the potentialities of human nature, and therefore, in the value of higher education as the indispensable means of realizing those potentialities. He has given us a nr faith in the democratic method of arriving at truth by agreement, and therefore in the value of reason, and in the necessity of participation in the democratic process. He has given us a new sense of the solidarity of mankind, and therefore of our need to put away childish things and to stand together in our common labors under the sun. And lastly he has kindled in our hearts and in the hearts of many thousands who have felt the warmth of his being an inextinguishable fire.

The concluding words of Professor Otto's response may fittingly bring to a close this biographical note. They can best be read against the backdrop of the address, already referred to, which he had made, a little more than a month earlier, before the Wisconsin branch of the American Association of University Professors. That address included this remark, which his audience found most disconcerting: "East and West among Wisconsin alumni, and among people who have known us only by reputation, the belief is growing that the social idealism and the pioneering spirit which made our university one of the great universities of America is not alive in us today." Here are Mr. Otto's final words at his Jubilee:

Education may be likened to a river. There come times in the life of a river when its banks are buried under the mud that has flowed down for miles. The mud dries into a crust and the life on its banks is buried under it, seemingly forever. But the rains fall, the winds blow, and the sun comes out. The hardened mud cracks open and fresh shoots appear. In due time the banks are again rimmed with green.

There is a great deal of talk all over the country about the mud that has settled down on the enterprise of education. This meeting shows that there is life in that enterprise. You are of the rain, the wind, and the sun. The mud will crack and education will grow again and be more meaningful—more full of vigor than ever.

Index